A Festival of New Black Poets in America

BlackSpirits

A Festival of New Black Poets in America

Edited by **WOODIE KING**

with Artistic Consultant **IMAMU AMIRI BARAKA**

Foreword by **NIKKI GIOVANNI**

Introduction by **DON L. LEE**

Random House *New York*

ISBN: 0-394-47620-4
Library of Congress Catalog Card Number: 79-37056

Grateful acknowledgment is extended to the following
publications in which these poems first appeared:
Black World: For "Albert Ayler: Eulogy for a Decomposed
Saxophone Player" by Stanley Crouch (August 1971); for "The Red,
Black and the Green" by S. E. Anderson (August 1971); "Where Have
You Gone" (February 1967), "A Good Assassination Should Be
Quiet" (May 1968), "Brother . . . the Twilight" (July 1968) by Mari Evans;
for "The Coming of John" by Amus Mor (September 1969); "You Are Alms"
by James Thompson (December 1967). *Journal of Black Poetry:* For
"Chain Waves" by S. E. Anderson. *Broadside Press:* For "To Anita,"
"To Morani and Mungu," "Don't Wanna Be," from *It's A New Day,
Poems for Young Brothas and Sistuhs* by Sonia Sanchez. Copyright ©
1971 by Sonia Sanchez; for "But He Was Cool," "Blackwoman," "Poem
Looking for a Reader" from *Don't Cry, Scream* by Don L. Lee. Copyright ©
1969 by Don L. Lee. *Third World Press:* For "Untitled," "Let's Go
Somewhere" by Johari Amini (1970); for "The Nation Is Like Ourselves"
by Imamu Amiri Baraka (LeRoi Jones) from *It's Nation Time* (1970); for
"Popsicle Cold," "Brothers the Struggle Must Go On," "Clairvoyance,"
"Mind and Soul After Dark" from *Destination Ashes* by Norman Jordan.
Black Creation: For "Queens of the Universe" by Sonia Sanchez.

Manufactured in the United States of America
By H. Wolff Book Co., N.Y.

9 8 7 6 5 4 3 2
First Edition

For Willie Mae King, Elma Lewis,
Esther Edwards and Esther Jackson

(4 dynamite blk women)

*Special acknowledgment to Sister Paula Giddings,
without whose help this book would not have happened.*

Foreword

There's always something about the changing of the seasons that gets next to me. The moon looks closer, the sun feels warmer, the trees smell greener, the pavement seems blacker—and we, a little older, a little wiser, with a little more love and a bit more patience, are in change also. Whether we go from summer to winter, spring to fall, a certain newness, a special freshness comes into play.

Autumn to me should always be spent in Nashville making love to some Meharry student who swears he never loved anyone the way he loves you. Winter is Cincinnati and running up and down the ice-covered hills at suicidal speeds in a beat up car that hasn't seen a heater in the last five years —making it to someone's apartment to watch the football game, drink beer, play cards and prepare our faces for the white masks we must wear the next five days to get back to the black end. It really doesn't matter where spring is spent as long as the clothes are loose and the eyes happy and the talk glib and the thoughts new. That's what the world is about—being new, because we as a people are in our spring-time.

And it's all so beautifully new and exciting—like the girl who lost her cherry and found a bang and really can't understand why she didn't do that years ago, not understanding that if she had done it years ago it couldn't have been nearly as good. One must prepare oneself for change, just as one must be prepared for love. It takes a full knowledge of options before one is ready to say, I Chose This.

No one who speaks of love can in the same breath speak of restricting options. When the team is winning, the ballpark is full; when the game is tight, everybody wants to play. And this is the point where the poet comes in. The poet can chronical where we as a people have been and where we'd like to go. But unlike the politician, the poet can give the vision and the space. The politician gives a vision that says, "If you follow me all your problems will be over," while the poet says, "If you understand where I'm coming from you will gain the tools to solve your own problems." And that's real. And reality is to be sought.

People are going to the moon and it's a good joke, but wouldn't it be cool if some little Black country in the heart of Mother Africa could send some Black man up there? The whole world is about change. When we wear traditional dress it's new to us—we take electricity and running water for granted. Other people do just the opposite. Which makes them neither right nor wrong, but seeking the things that are newest for them. And the question is whether we will allow each his own genesis, his own alpha?

The newest people on earth are Afro-Americans. Our genesis is the blending of the old with the new. And our task is to keep both ovens alight without either of them catching fire. Through the centuries Afro-Americans have had to develop a certain tolerance for difference, which is one of our strengths. We recognize old people do things the old ways; yet we neither praise the summer for being hot, nor curse the winter for its cold. And as we move toward new strengths we even appreciate the restlessness spring brings to us. And that's when we read a poem by a poet who loves, not us because he doesn't know us, but himself because he knows himself. For all that he is. Or might never be.

NIKKI GIOVANNI

August 1971

[x]

Contents

[xiv]

Words in the Early Time:
An Introduction

In the Sixties when the words came in the early time, they ripped and tore at our insides/outsides while forcing some of us into the back rooms of our beginning. A few advanced minds said that the future saw the poets even though the poets didn't see it. These poets, these brothers and sisters flashed on to this earth with an advantage other "poets" didn't possess; they were *really* brothers and sisters. At this point in time, their humanity, their feelings toward each other had not been altered by the killers: the evils of competition, of becoming known, had not invaded their youthfulness. After all, the poets were all fighting the same war, but like ill-trained guerillas, they were soon to find out that few of them had any knowledge of the war games.

New Air/Same Historical Breeze:

Check your vision young Africans. What part of the world do you prefer? Is it the museums of Paris on a Guggenheim; they say that if you really want to study African art you *must* go to europe where 90% of it is on display as memories of the realworld. Is it the land of highgrass and full sun inhabited by like-images of yourselves where brothers and sisters die daily trying to recapture their own? Or is it the land of buildings that scrape the sky where you just bend with the wind and reflect the power of others while imitating the dirtiness of the european consciousness? Listen, young Africans, for our purposes there are more similarities, between a Harlem and a Zimbabwe, than differences; they are both occupied by blackpeople and both ruled from the outside; both explode with black energy and both are at war with the worldrunners. Is there really a choice? Samuel Yette doesn't think so. And who needs the negro? Certainly not Sidney Wilhelm. The important decisions were made in the late Thirties and early Forties as to what to do with us.

However, if you understand the early time, understand the days of the black renaissance, maybe you'll begin to realize that what's happening today in Chicago, New York, San Francisco, New Orleans (in part) had its origin in the Harlem of the Twenties. Yesterday's renaissance was, by and large, restricted to Harlem, restricted to the artists, writers, musicians, entertainers, and the whites who supported and patronized the participants. The masses of blacks in Harlem knew little of the raging young voices, but some were kept informed through the vehicles of the *Crisis* and *Opportunity* magazines. The majority of the *big* night clubs did not openly solicit the patronage of Harlemites for fear that their presence might affect the flow of whites from other parts of New York. Other acts of subtle exclusion existed in all the arts which aided in the renaissance's popularity among whites rather than blackpeople.

These were the years of Marcus Garvey, the black giant from the West Indies who first lit the fire and turned black eyes toward black Africa. His "back to Africa" cries initiated the first mass black nationalist movement to hit this country. The motion of Garvey's U.N.I.A. helped give impetus to the young poets. We see our images in the work of Langston Hughes' " Afro-American Fragment":

> So long
> So far away
> Is Africa.

Not even memories alive
Save those that history books create,
Save those that songs
Beat back into the blood—
Beat out of blood with words sad-sung
In strange un-Negro tongue—
So long,
So far away
Is Africa.

We had the deadly vision of Claude McKay whose *Home to Harlem* was a best seller and upset the black bourgeoisie with its realness and gut-level dialogue. McKay's poetry struck home too with lines like:

If we must die, let it not be like hogs
Hunted and penned in an inglorious spot,
While round us bark the mad and hungry dogs,
Making their mock at our accursed lot.

W. E. B. DuBois covered every area with his prestigious output. His presence is felt in history, sociology, and education, as well as literature. However, one of his greatest contributions was as editor of *Crisis* magazine where in April of 1915 he stated:

In art and literature we should try to loose the tremendous emotional wealth of the Negro and the dramatic strength of his problems through writing, the stage, pageantry, and other forms of art. We should resurrect forgotten ancient Negro art and history, and we should set the black man before the world as both a creative artist and a strong subject for artistic treatment.

DuBois was not only strong in his prose: his poetry, too, was able to move inactive minds. Listen to "A Litany at Atlanta" written in 1906 after a race riot in Atlanta:

> Who made these devils? Who nursed them
> in crime and fed them on injustice? Who
> ravished and debauched their mothers and
> their grandmothers? Who bought and sold
> their crime, and waxed fat and rich on
> public iniquity?

There were other voices, such as Sterling Brown's:

> They weigh the cotton
> They store the corn
> We only good enough
> to work the rows;
> We run the commissary
> They keep the books
> We gotta be grateful
> For being cheated.

Fenton Johnson stated:

> I am tired of work;
> I am tired of building up somebody else's civilization

While Countee Cullen sang:

> Yet do I marvel at this curious thing;
> To make a poet black, and bid him sing!

Much of this insight and truth was recorded for us in Alain Locke's historic anthology *The New Negro*. And black poets such as James Weldon Johnson, Jean Toomer, Melvin B. Tolson, Frank Horne, and Arna Bontemps were to lead us into the Thirties and Forties to such voices as Frank Marshall Davis, whose free verse burst with newness, to Richard Wright who is primarily known as a novelist, but whose "Between the World and Me" would not let us forget the hanging tree. Robert Hayden, while denying his "negroness," especially in his poetry, still impressed us with such masterpieces as "Runagate, Runagate," "Middle Passage," "Homage to the Empress of the Blues," and "Frederick Douglass." Yes, we had the writers, the ideas and direction, but we didn't have the doers, the people who take the words and play follow-up.

Something went wrong. Drastically wrong. Tell me somebody—anybody, please, what happened? If we produced/created the only indigenous music in this country, *why* don't we control it, why don't we own more record companies? If we've produced the *real* music, why aren't *we the authorities*? Why are we not writing all the books and newspaper columns? Why is it that the Leonard Feathers, Dan Morgensterns, Nat Hentoffs, and Martin Williamses are living in style off *our* music, and our best musicians are forced to feed their veins with words of praise and stupid smiles? Miles Davis is not great because some pseudo-jazz critic said so—Miles is great because he worked and suffered and prepared himself for greatness. That goes for Duke, Count, Monk, Cecil, Ella, Billie, Coltrane, and countless others that made black music what it is. We made the music and the enemy owns it! What came out of the first renaissance other than the words and musical notes that we can say we own? Did we build any mass publishing companies? Did we build any distributing companies? We know about the record companies, but do we even own the copyrights? What institutions did we create—what lifegiving, lifesaving institutions did the Harlem Renaissance initiate?

Yeah, we fell into the Thirties and Forties and almost got slain again with the new "worker's" ideology: *Workers of the World Unite.* Along came the communists, now known as the old left, and some of the poets and intelligentsia actually began to believe that the Marxists could do what we're supposed to do ourselves—could solve all our problems—and they actually forced some of the poets and writers to believe that the answers had nothing to do with race, but with the inequality of the classes. Thus it was that the whole African consciousness which originated in the Twenties was almost lost because "race literature" was frowned upon as "black racism." This "black racism" was also thrown at brothers and sisters who felt that their identity had to be preserved through some form of nationalism. Yet, the jewish nationalists worked actively for their causes and the w.a.s.p. nationalists ruled the communist party with their brand of international nationalism. It was the black poets who first acted with any kind of independence. Ray Durem relates his experience this way:

> There was, however, a period in my life when I hoped that by building left-wing organizations without respect to color, we could do away with the rank injustice in the states. At the end of World War II, I discovered that even the white radicals were not interested in a radical solution to the Negro question. Perhaps the development in my thinking and writing can be summed up as follows: I lived many years thinking to teach the American white man. I discovered that the task is to kill him!

If Durem's words are not enough, check out Richard Wright's essay in *The God That Failed,* and for the real doubters, glance over the last days of W. E. B. DuBois; and tell me, what has happened to Paul Robeson? And to the opposite, the *right* ain't never been right either. The right has not been as subtle as the left in wholesale co-optation of "negroes." All this is to say that in the final analysis the ideologies of the white left and the white right are just two hands on the same body being manipulated by the same white brain. While the mind of the european-american was not adverse to outright physical force, their most effective weapon was to appeal to the "intelligence" of the "negro" spokesmen through the careful and insidious use of twentieth-century rhetoric.

They Talked A Good Talk: The Rhetoricians

The white boy's use of words and the negro's naiveté in believing most of them has contributed greatly to our present predicament. It is possible that all out war between blacks and whites in this country would have long ago been operative if we hadn't taken words like the United States' constitution with its bill of rights seriously, if we hadn't listened to the jewish and anglo-saxon liberals and believed that our cause was their cause, that our fight was their fight. After all, there were no negroes heading any jewish or anglo-saxon organizations, but the Jews were the strong voices in everything we had from the early C.O.R.E., S.N.C.C., N.A.A.C.P., S.C.L.C. to the present day Black Panthers.

The europeans talked their way into leading us to *our* freedom—as if it wasn't they from whom we were trying to get free. The masters of rhetoric fooled many. Ronald Steel puts it this way:

> The rhetoric so many of us grew up on was designed to lull us to sleep. It assured us that our motives were pure, our actions noble, our ambitions self-denying. It told us that our society, while not perfect, was the nearest thing to perfection man had achieved—and that it was getting better every day. It taught us that "liberty and justice for all," meant all, not just for

whites and those who could afford a lawyer, or a doctor, or the price of a decent education. It also told us
that Americans were being sent out to die so that
freedom might live in such places as Korea, Vietnam, Cuba, and the Dominican Republic. But we
have learned that another word for that kind of freedom is counterrevolution.

Yes, the wordusers and their actual actions were going in
different directions. Up into the Sixties, we believed things
would get better, and like butter on a hot fire the negro
would melt in; into *what* was never really asked or analyzed
because the fight left the South, and we came North where
we thought we could win. We got burnt. Addison Gayle, Jr.,
wrote:

> Here in the North, rhetoric and practice come into
> conflict. It is no surprise that the great rhetoricians
> of America are Northerners, for here rhetoric is the
> most celebrated avocation. From the politician in the
> highest echelon of Government to the freshman col-
> lege student come the wail of discontent, the table
> thumping oratory, the endless reports of committees,
> civil rights groups, civic organizations, all attesting
> to the deep concern, the great sympathy felt by men
> of the North, more sophisticated, more liberal, for
> their fellow citizens who happen to be black.

And for the citizen who happens to be black, the doctor who
happens to be black, the lawyer who happens to be black,
the teacher, the minister, and the anything that happens to
be black, the rhetoric *worked*. Yet, to some, a few—those of
us who had heard Malcolm X and listened, to those who
knew the usefulness of our history and knew it didn't start
here, to those for whom critical and subjective thinking
existed as a natural part of themselves, to those who could

see above the rhetoric and who knew deep down in their innards that we were Africans and not some imitation europeans, to those new brothers and sisters who were tired of being hip slaves singing "Oh Happy Days" in the latest european rock fashion, it was necessary to begin to dance to their own beat. This beat was picked up and led in part by the new blackpoets.

The New Black Renaissance

Hoyt W. Fuller, the perceptive editor of *Black World* magazine (which replaced *Crisis* magazine as the most important communicating device used by the new poets) named the new period. Hoyt Fuller in his own quiet way gave direction to the new movement and helped found the Organization of Black American Culture in Chicago. He became the advisor to its Writers' Workshop. Writers such as Ebon, Carolyn Rodgers, Zubena, David Llorens, Cecil Brown, Sam Greenlee, Sterling D. Plumpp, Johari M. Amini, Ronda Davis, Alicia L. Johnson, and Don L. Lee give thanks to O.B.A.C. for the help it has contributed to their growth. Many of them are still active members, helping and giving direction to the younger writers. John O. Killens, one of our most noted and published novelists, left Brooklyn and went South to Fisk University to coordinate its writing program and initiated its annual writers' conference that was always stimulating and helpful. Under Killens and the Fisk Writers' Workshop we acquired poets Donald L. Graham and Nikki Giovanni.

The West Coast gave us a couple of black quarterlies. The Journal of Black Poetry, under the untiring editorship of Joe Goncalves, being the most persistent and productive. (At this writing sixteen issues have been produced at an average of about three a year.) The other journal was

Soul Book which also published many of the new and on-coming poets. The West Coast gave us Stanley Crouch, Askia Muhammad Toure (by way of New York), Jon Eckels, Marvin X, Bob Kaufman, Carol Freeman, Everett Hoagland, and the Black Panthers.

The Midwest produced three publishing companies: Broadside Press, Third World Press, and Free Black Press. Broadside Press, the largest and most productive, published almost everybody: Ahmed Alhamisi, Nikki Giovanni, Doughtry Long, Marvin X, Dudley Randall, Frenchy Hodges, Jon Eckels, Margaret Danner, James A. Emanuel, Etheridge Knight, Margaret Walker, Keorapetse Kgositsile, Barbara Mahone, Sonia Sanchez, Don L. Lee, and was able to pull Gwendolyn Brooks away from Harper and Row. Broadside Press mainly concentrated its efforts in the field of black poetry with about forty-two books for its listing. Broadside, under the direction of Dudley Randall, has now moved into criticism, posters, tapes, and anthologies. If Broadside can hold on to its writers, I feel they'll have a strong publishing house that can stand up to anyone in the late Seventies—early Eighties.

Third World press, which not only publishes poetry, but fiction, non-fiction, and children's books, continues to break new ground. Among its authors are Carolyn M. Rodgers, Johari M. Amini, Sterling D. Plumpp, Ebon, Keorapetse Kgositsile, Askia Muhammad Toure, Imamu Amiri Baraka (who is the acknowledged "Father" of the present day black arts movement), Charlie Cobb, Ifeanyi Menkiti, Zack Gilbert, Dudley Randall, Philip Royster, and Sam Greenlee. In its non-fiction series, Third World Press has published Hoyt W. Fuller, St. Clair Drake (in cooperation with the Institute of the Black World), Dr. George Kent, Mari Evans, Gwendolyn Brooks, Luevester Lewis, and others. Third World Press in the Seventies focuses its attention on "books for the living," directing its editorial policy toward the creation of a black world consciousness.

The East Coast saw the creation of Drum and Spear Press in Washington, D.C., and Jihad Productions in New Ark in the late Sixties. In 1970 we also got the Black Academy Press in Buffalo, Emerson Hall in New York, and the Third Press, also in New York. Drum and Spear, at this writing, is the most productive, concentrating its efforts on African literature and children's books. Jihad has published brothers like the honorable Julius Nyerere, Imamu Amiri Baraka and has plans to publish brothers like Sékou Touré, and Kwame Nkrumah in the near future.

There are probably other publishing institutions that I've failed to mention but you should get the idea by now. By and large, the poets published in and directed their voices to the black community only. In essence, in terms of any public attention, they were noticed first in the black communities. They were a fundamental part of the community they spoke of.

In his widely read and sometimes wrongly used *The Wretched of the Earth*, Frantz Fanon divided the literature of colonized people into three periods: (1) the assimilationist phase, (2) the pre-combat literature, and (3) the fighting phase where "instead of according the people's lethargy an honored place in his esteem, [the author] turns himself into an awakener of the people; hence comes a fighting literature, a revolutionary literature and a national literature. During this period a great many men and women who up till then would never have thought of producing a literary work, now that they find themselves in exceptional circumstances, feel the need to speak to their nation, to compose the sentence which expresses the heart of the people and to become the mouthpiece of a new reality in action." To paraphrase Margaret Walker, we had become believers in ourselves. We didn't need any white boys to tell us if we could write. Anyway, unlike black music, black literature had produced black critics. Along with the new poets we got new critics. Larry Neal jumped out there in *Liberator;* Darwin T. Turner and Dr. George Kent graced the pages of the *C.L.A. Journal* and other periodicals; Addison Gayle, Jr., and Stephen E. Henderson proved to be most prolific. James A. Emanuel and Richard Long made the transition from the old into the new and Carolyn Rodgers and Carolyn Gerald enlarged us all with their insight and beauty in the pages of *Black World*. These critics and others agreed with Imamu Baraka in that "there is no objective anything." They didn't completely detach themselves from the literature. They knew they were a part and refused to play white boy with some pseudo-objectivity. All of this led Addison Gayle, Jr., to say:

> We are today in a Black cultural renaissance, in which for perhaps the last time, Black Nationalist writers will be able to project—to Black people—a sense of our unique, separate cultural identity by resolving the dichotomy between art and function, thereby making art functional and relevant to the Black community.

These poets have a lot going for them. They were made by the black community, and made known by the black press. For once we control our own art form—the feeling is good.

DON L. LEE

Writer-in-residence
Howard University
September, 1971

JOHARI AMINI

Signals

is yo eye so empty
in the moonlight of yo smoke
u cant see me waitin
for u to sway my way
sway fine & black & o so cool
a swift swayin tree
swayin bendin down
& catchin me up into yo movement
pleasin u?
is yo eye so empty
in the moonlight of yo smoke
u cant see me waitin

o my man
our beginning will be
as beginnings be
total through all the sweet secretions
from your prime cause

and i will be a womanfire
orbiting your night

and you will protect my burning softness
because you wont be

out
of
it
when i need you

Untitled

(in commemoration of the blk/family)

we will be no generashuns to cum for blks r
killing r.selves did u hear bros.did u hear the
killings did u hear the sounds of the killing
the raping of the urgency of r soil consuming
r own babies burned n the acid dri configura-
shuns of the cycles balancing did u hear.did u
hear. hear the sounds of the balancing &
checking off checking off erasing r existence
from the count of the cosmos while r mother
moans for the loss of r funkshun & who we
will never be did u hear bros.hear .hear.hear
the sounds of r mother of her moaning as she
moans while we allow her to lie stretch ing
herself from Dakar to Dar es Salaam & she
moans & tears her flesh & gushes did u hear
the gushing bros.did u hear.hear.did u hear
the sounds of the gushing oil from her members spraying the auto mated powers of a
foreign god who ruts in.to her did u hear the
sounds.sounds.bros.sounds of the rutting did
u hear.hear did u hear the rutting of the
animal with the golden hair rutting in.to her
urgency eating the sacrificied & futile fetuses
erupted n the fascinated juices of the cycles
of pills which will control the number of her
mouths did u hear.did u hear the cycles
turning bros.did u hear them we will be no
mor . . .

S. E. ANDERSON

The Sound of Afro-American Music
Chapt. 1

The history of blacklife is put down in the motions
of mouths and blackhands with fingering lips
and puckered raven fingers bluesing the air of
today and eeking out the workgrunts   getting down
to earth   the nittygritty   i mean   they mean:
you dig and if you don't don't you worry pretty
momma   we all feel dat way anyway   and sister
it's a pity whitey done this to us but I love you
and my history says whitey ain't shit and should be flushed
but poppa and momma may have the 'ligion but god don't
mean a thing baby when you got no bread and a bed
and a bad head blinding you with blackblues of gospel
bashing out of the bigblack
sisters' lips spiritually into the bop and now the
avantgarde jazz of a hard shepp and blackblues looking over
hunched hardworked shoulders into the sepia polyrhythmic
soil: lord, lord we done come far and still ain't nowhere
near even with long nappy hair and talk of revolution . . .
jumpin with my bro   you know   out there in
dolphyland or baby maybe into that sun-ra shit beautiful but
bars are 8 & 12 like dinah and luther king digging malcolm
shinin in my front door   sweet momma keepin kisses for
my high with fontella & 'retha takin care of much business
                in the rhythm of the blues

[6]

Chain Waves

I went to Riis Beach and Put my ear to the ocean
I went to Atlantic City and Put my ear to the ocean
I went to Chesapeake Bay and Put my ear to the ocean

I went to the South Sea Islands and put my ear to
                                     clapboardwalls

I heard chains inside the ocean's roar
I heard Bones whitened by salty time rattlin for blackskin
I heard defiant moanblues in Yoruba, Ibo, Akan, Bantu

I heard transformed memories and tears drop from ashy
                                    seaswept faces

I looked into jamestown waters and saw
Blackbones beckoning me in rhythm to a Jr. Walker wail
I looked into Savannah waters and saw
Blackhusbands hugging sister/mothers crying—cradling
                                    their unborn
I looked into the Everglades and Bayou Swamps and saw
rusted rifles clenched by deathfists fortelling Brother Nat

I looked through clapboardwalls and saw
Gabriel's ghost whispering Revolt in my ears.

II

In the Sunrise East no winds blew
        but the sea was restless
In the Sunrise East no clouds passed
        but the air darkened—
        anticipating war
In the Sunrise East I looked behind me :
        the skyline America with brothers
        and sisters taking their places

In the Sunrise East no shadows prevailed
just mahogany memorybones salted and searching
for ebonyflesh in Revenge and Humanity

III

and now our bonebrothers feel
it is time that they rise up :
we had called for them in our ancestral wails
through Bessie, Shine, Nina, Tbone, Curtis . . .

And now our fleshless fighters make
the tide rise inspite of the whitemoon

we had fought without Them and within Them
now we fight with Them as Them as Us.

and now Black Bonetide *rise!* crackling
against Carib shores and Bahia—
defying the arrogant Lunalust
pulling against the Namibian and Azanian shores.

The flaming chain waves of our unity with all of us
cut the invisible shackles of moontide
flooding the steelglass caves and canyons of the
                                    Snowpeople
melting the Deathsoul into Sodomdeath
Roasting their maggotthoughts clearing the Earth's air
for us to breathe and recreate
what Coltrane spearwhispered to us—Spiritual Unity
what Shango kept chanting to Campos—Liberation
for us to breathe and recreate
what Allah hummed to Malcolm—Self-Determination
for us to breathe and recreate Okra and Nommo
                              and Peace

The Red   The Black   &   The Green

The Red

for the death to life leaps of the Middle Passage
for the Freedomflames of our fathers Gabriel and Nat
for the Contraband: Harriet Tubmanbrave
for the Bluesglue binding our battered souls

for Billy and the Strange Fruit hanging hanging from hate
for Nina and the children leaning, leaning for love

for the Red of our Passion and Revenge.

The Black

for the Brothers resurrected from the Nod.
for the Sisters reborn from the Trick
for the Rebellions: dress rehearsals for the funeral of ofays
for the Afro-crowned Foxes Bustin forth Everywhere

for the continuence of chittlins and death to the pig!
for the Jennie Lou and Junebug for surviving

for our Magicians with their Ju-Ju and Mojo growing
        warriors
                        in the soil of our Souls

for the Black of our bodies poised in the Unity of Liberation.

The Green

for our land called America, Africa, Caribbean
for our Earth-good-after the white plague—like before
for our Nommowaters flowing in the lovedance creating
        our futures
for our laughter of colors against our oppression

for our parents birthing us into the War for Humanity
for Coltranism, leonopolis and Pharaoh for deepening our
        Spiritual Unity
for Garvey, Campos and Che and Dessalines who touch us
        and guide us
                through the ancestoral chants of Rhythm
                      and Blues

for the Black Kingdom and the Power and the Glory of
        Black People

        For All Praises Are Due To The Blackman

           for Peace
           Forever

IMAMU AMIRI BARAKA

Somebody's Slow Is
Another Body's Fast   ((*Preachment*))

Somebody's slow is another body's fast
how fast we gon travel, to get up outta here
how fast can we move to move on way from this jive
how quick can we slick, how quick can we untrick
our slick self, dazzled by devils, shining weights on
our knees, tricks is good, say a trick, nick, he's a hip
kid sells his mama's children dope for a green vine,
cool in hell, cool cool cool. Somebody's fast is no
food at all, stalled on the lowway with all our toll
gol ripped off by unconscious pieces of our self. My
heart, my love, my shriveled mind, my eye, my touch,
my feeling, all hurdle and float, they out on the block,
they on different sides of the street. On different sides
of the question, "allahu akbar" over here, "right on"
over there, "habari gani" all up in around where i
am, and we still, all of us, somebody's slow stool for
muddy feet. The bloody foot-claws of a beast, squash
our naked brain. Blood, and mud, mix with brown
grey brain meat. The sparks droop, the fire wilts,
mud images and blood images. Yusef says we are
frankenstein dancing to the music of a Mad souless
beast. But its our music. Its our rhythm. Its our
sound and fury. We hip and fast. We travel without
touchin the ground. Dig me Dig me Dig me. We say.
But thats all we say. Dig me Dig me its a putt putt
sound to DraculaPig teeth rippin black sky's blood.

On the way to cool moon Dracula Pig Teeth on the
way to cooooool moooooooon. We gotta get faster if
fast will do it. We gotta be slicker if slick gonna get it.
Here's a slick trick to us in a green cadillac a green hat
a green suit a green finger nail file and green dirt
underneath green finger nails. He's green and hes
mean clean as somebody humping his mama for 300
years can sell it to you sell it to you buy it nigger buy
it, can sell or give or make you believe anything. I'm
god up here on the wall. Dumb ass nigger. I'm super
smart having created even you from a higher form of
life the african which you now hate . . . . . hehe-
hehehehehehehehehehe . . . . can you understand . . . . a higher form of life . . heh heh heh
heh heh . . . .
We are fast alright.
We better fast . . . lay off hogknuckles stuffed
with cocaine and whitemagic Lay off savages' flute
farts for loud silence to cool the fool slave Cool The
Fool Slave. Give him job. Here. Give him white lady.
Here. Give him ideology. Here. Give him magic
hatred of everything strong in him. Here. Cool The
Fool Slave Here Monkey, jump up and down. OK
throw fist up in air, say power to the people. Here.
Good.Ja whol my man. OK all those who dont want
to get shot straight out just crawl up in visionary
bedrooms with negative aspects of the shadow and
call our name every five seconds till you change.
Here. Every Five Second.s God. Jesus. Darwin. Marx.

Marcuse. Here. Whhhh Whhhh Whhhh Whhh Whhh
Yes. Whhhhh. Right. Whhhhh. On. Whhhhh
Yeh (nods, droops, scratches) Yeh. Whhhh. (Snorts.)

We are very slow. See. Very slow. Get up.
We are not moving. I want warmth. Heat me. Get up.
See. Move. Very slow. Go faster. We are in our hip
terribleness so cool yet slow. A rocket bursts past our
face killing our whole history. The sphinx our father
squats in the desert waiting to be caught up with. We
are very slow, he says. Unmoving to make us dig
ourselves. Pharaoh, listen to Jr. Walker. Jr. Walker.
listen to the silence of the desert. James Brown read
Mwalimu Nyerere. Staple Singers read A Black Value
System. We are very slow. Listen. A breath, murmur
ancient one hum pick up rhythm rock a ceiling of
sun our selves rising birth.
Are we alive
Yes. But we are barely moving. Too Slow. Go ahead
brother move.

Go ahead me you. Be us.
Head speak to hand. Leg respond. I love. Feel
Ohhhh. Feel. Here I am
Touch me. Pull it all in hear. Hear
I weeee. Bee weeee. A weeeeee. Us need. Us. Us need.
our self's. Us cd be, big as sea, big as we, we big, we
love. Feel. Head know eye. Eye. See. Ear. Hear, Hand,
what you doing. Doing. Are you doing. That's njema,
hand. Call foot mouth, tell him to pick up. Call heart

to pump food to fist. Yeabo. Move. That's hip, njema. Njema. Hofu ni kwenu, we whisper along the veins of black existence. Hofu ni kwenu, along all beautifuling chords of black life, my fear, my love, my fear, is for you, us, we us, only i to make black, weusi, njema, hofu ni kwenu. . . . a call like the wonderful ripples of eternal water, carrying the touching of mungu roho, holyspirit, can the outside reach the inside, holy consciousness, can the sidewalk, talk to the black ghost of love. Vibration soft thunder, jagged edge of always terrible perfection, touch touch, speak pamoja, unison. One word. One sound. One final, never always, its not is, the one, ooooooo, alll, the circle, what, see, see, you can we are, the bee the beee, to beee, the all, the alll, ooooooooo, spirit spirit spirit spirit . . . .
And what is left is moving constant tremble lifes alive
Can we raise ourselves. Increased the vibration. The cycle of life to constant frequency.

> All is
> none is

constant.
It is all vibration
The swing of endless pendulum
I want we.
We as the two extremes oned.
Atone.
A   Z   one strike forever moving
claaaaaaaaaaaaaaannnnnnnggg
Clang in us

A   Z   oned atone.
We are a man meditating. We are bodies moving together in love. We are communities looking into the
sky for a moment on the clear way to liberation. We
are cities readying brothers to lead us. We are nation,
great body, collect the fragments of the milky way,
aswirl a top our heads, where thru the cosmic voice
like perfect jagged steel stabs in stabs in the be
the be
and we
will be

The Nation Is Like Ourselves

The nation is like our selves, together
Seen in our various scenes, sets where ever we are
what ever we are doing, is what the nation
is
doing
or
not doing
is what the nation
is
being
or
not being

Our nation sits on stoops and watches airplanes take off
our nation is kneeling in the snow bleeding through 6 layers
of jewish enterprise
our nation is standing in line ashamed in its marrow for
                                                    being
our nation
a people without knowledge of itself
dead matter we are thrown on the soil to richen
european fields
the dead negro is fertilizer
for the glorious western harvest

our nation is ourselves, under the steel talons
of the glorious

Devil
our secret lover who tells us what to do
the steel orange eyes
the ripping fingers of
the Devil
who tells us what to do
blondie
your dress so high
wallachs nigger
mod nigger
nigger in a cow boy hat
why you want to be a cow boy
laid up with a cow

he shouts "power to the nipples,"
doctor nigger, please do some somethin on we
lawyer nigger, please pass some laws about us
liberated nigger with the stringy haired mind, please lib lib
lib
you spliv er ate
US, we you, coo-
lust dancing thru yr wet look
ing
tent
acles
please mister liberated nigger love chil   nigger
nigger in a bellbottom bell some psychodelic wayoutness
on Yo People, even while you freeing THE People, please

just first free YO people, ol marijuana jesus I dug your last
      record
with the hootenany biscuits, was revolutionary as a
      motherfucker, ple
ple please mister kinkyman, use your suntan susan swartz is
      using
it, her and tom jones on their show with you and diane
      carroll tiny ti
mmm and the newest negro to understand that theres no
      black no white
only people . . .
      yo imagination is fabulous, reverend, pray for color
      peeples, when the mayor or after the mayor or before
      duh mayor give you yo check, please reverend, and
        daddyboy
and tonto greengrits, and pablo douchebag, susan goldberg's
      daring
nongringo, and allthekidstogather . . . reach back to the
      constant silence
in our lives, where the ideas line up to be graded, and get a
      better one
going than we got, for you and me,
please mr new thing
please mr mystical smasheroo just under ¼ strength
      learning about it
from the flying dutchman
please mr ethnic meditations professor profess your love for
      black

people we waiting
while you say right on and commit the actual take over of
        yourself
in the anteroom of anything, just before or just after
        anything
truudging down the halls of your wives straightened haid we
        realize
how tough things are and how you cant alienate the people
        with the
money we live among stars and angels, listen to devils
        whines like
cold space between the planets, we know
the turn in the hall, your visit to the phone booth to put on an
inferior man suit
a super animal trump
the tarts of your individual consciousness
please all you individuals
and would be involved if people were nicer to you types
or frightened of the military aspects of national liberational
        folks
in your reinvolved consciousness flitting over the sea at
        jamaica
if the rastafarians dont kill you please mr vacationing writer
        man
write some heavy justice
about black people
we waiting
we starved for your realness
we know you on the move now
we heard you was outside cairo

bathing at a spa
please mr world travler
please mr celebrity, mr nigger in the treasury department
mr disc jockey for the mournful cash register of the nigger
          soul
please mr all of us
please miss lady bug
oh lady or brother, wherever and who ever you are
breathing on
oh please please in the night time
more please in the mewning
we need need you bbbaby man, we need all the blood we
          gotta
get some blood and
you in your wilderness blood
is the nigger
yes the sweet lost nigger
     you are our nation sick ass assimilado
          please come back
               like james brown say
                    please please please

Move!

The job of criminals
((In our World)) is to disrupt the living
    cancerize the healthy
    introduce what shd not even be thought
              of
    but here in a criminals world
    the role of criminals is to be correct all
           the time
    and too powerful to mess with
    the job of criminals is the same but here
          it is legitimized
    and we are loud insane men in garish
          homemade suits
    and criminals are quiet well tailored
         gentlemen correct in the
    padded silence of really elegant clubs
    and criminals amongst us why we think
        of them as friends
    we will give them money, and allegiance,
        we will give them our
    very hearts, our lives
    and they, these friend micro crooks
      small fry in a world of richard
      nixons
      these brothers to us

cobulwarks against hells hot lip
they will be bs'sing all the while
    brother
they will be sliding, and lying,
    and screwing disease insects
they will be scraping all the men
    in the checker bd gutter
they will be stupid in spite of
    their words
they will be obstruction to pro-
    gress having arrived at what
    they think is heaven
and you will be almost helpless
    against them so close will
    they be
and you will throw up yr hands
    and try to weep and the tears
not coming will turn to knives in
    your head and endanger yr
    boiling brain
and they will go on and on being
    right being good men being
    followers of what is righteous
followers of what is black and hip
and they will be the fire-wood
    pretending to be the fire
and they will be the doodoo tell-
    ing people they are food

and what
will we do
                what shd we do

                look into the eyes of
                        the blackest
                        child
                and listen to the speech
                        the images (in
                        his eyes) make
                and you will under-
                        stand
                how simple in the
                        future
                the complex present
                is laughingly run down

The Spirit of Creation Is Blackness

Whatever happens we know
we've lived continue stream
of fire, zagged airburn showup
baby you me a star, get together
with the purest magnetism. We are
sons drawing new life go, together, as
part of the same. Inside outside, burn the
same, dawn, sunset, climb a rope robed
animal disappear the same. Scramble up
the pyramid. Halleleujah among the pyramids.
Preach an scream and dance atop the pyramid.
Salute yr father the sphinx His lions legs and bulls
body. His African patience to cool it so long out in
the sand, to teach a bunch of ovyo bloods wandering
around the world. But what ever's gonna happen its
happening. Look hand fist a torch shoved above our
head. And we can see. The way we moved drawn on
by our selves' hot looks. The heads a projector please
turn it to fast motion smiling so silent in the dark
amidst the images, when they come out they melt
the snow show us where to go and we on the road
already, we are our roads you know Your brain cd
catch your head on fire and it skeet fire like on a
weird calendar around yr television knot. Itd be
screaming look dig this something outside about to
spring, and you better come warm yourself by my

screamin knot. You never seen nobody cd walk around with they haid on fire and still sing the blues. But these are the reds, the greens the holy blacks of the necessary harmony. And theyd come all those who survived the snows cd hear or see or feel the umchababy sizz thru um, wd turn from the bullshit they was doing and stumble, move on over to where we was campin out in motion like the emotional erector set of flesh and spirit. Institutions of Blackness AntiSlavery brigade blowin hot changes for the advertised season comin comin And they'd come, bea bunch, a nation of em, yo head, our head be burnin so bad be burnin so good, wd light up where we was the world cd see and blind niggers be Missionary blackmen rightaway and walk across their watery chains reconstruct their whited out brains, and do the rhythmpop slow in fast glisten like the jewelry they digs, shine out like the hippopotamous topped alligator wheeled Funkmobiles they invented, for the movements sake, for the sounds sake, for the screech and tiptoes sake, for the colors sake, for the ahhaaahahahahahahaha's sake, and the yehman's sake, and digit's sake and the yougotit's sake, and the youthinkso huh's sake, and the sake of the shadow that drags along envying the body of the blood he longs to climb into unity with us and our father the son who are in the safe and peaceful place. (We lean across the space of meeting, say yeh, go head, do what you gotta do. its alright. the sun come up, most likely . . . and everything'll be all right. . . .

Yo head be all our heads and its risen like it was the
the sun drawn you up with it, and we are drawn
around in tune like motion, plane you plane me are
plane we, a crowd of us, swahili black, weusi jua,
and there are words with this melody, and words and
melody, tune, rhythm, the harmony, are all
the same,
we merge with it
all things are it
we rhythm and sound and suncolor
we rise and set and sing and move
oh lord, oh lord, oh lord. . . . . .

African Love History

chakadoopah
chakadoopow
chakadak chakadak chakadak
chatadoo chatadoo chataadoo
and on rhythm rage spirit stage
the grace of black men demanding they be god
that we all all in sane's way
in the human universe the spiritual circle to be
bow
bow
doom da doom da
padoo padoo padoo
in sane's light, against the almighty gobbling shadow
old colorless greedy shadow
eating amidst the scarlet and yellow horns
the hunchedback po' women
amidst the love we would build in the world
raging line of horns like black sovereigns humbled
before the sun's spirituality
Whoooowheee doodeedah doodeedah uwahuwahu
uwahuwahu uwahuwahu
against the sun's light we are the emerging future
life of the planet
the evolving species raising the very values of the
place,

all should be rulers submitting to
each other. all should be prophets
creating recreating evolving reevolving
the starry space wool divine
as the life of love and the hereafter of love the
energy content and form of all that remains or ever
really was is love, is love i wondered why my swift
brothers were lovers sang and created as they moved
love images even in the beastfull corridors total ice
hell, they are love, and we are love reachin for itself
trying to be itself
to love we love its love all love you love
the energy the wisdom the color of life is love
the form of the world
the sperm of the world
the rhythm and feel of the world
is love
what we need and move in our conscious stretchout
                                                    love
you see the economy
the politics, the natural order
or actual men
of the men who raise themselves above the corpses
of extinct monsters we donot condemn cave men but
life shd not be condemned to be in caves forever
Leave them in the snow with the bloody meat, Let
the Pope and Adolph Hitler and Hoover squat over
newly found fire at the shadow show of licking salty

stubs. The mad snow rituals will get Bill Basie and Satchmo high, will force the new music. The snow children will wear our colors and mouth the sound of the new learning. And the new learning will raise them so they slay their beast like fathers, striving to be men. The work of the world is constant and beautiful. Husks of dinosaurs, Huge skulls sucked on by invisible animals. Invisible men. All the hosts of the many lords in the love image one, and our nation but a soul spread out to be filled by the newly conscious the newly righteous to lift the whole race of men who can be lifted, the created for newness, the survivors of the death trap cave world. The fleers and beers past square grey body-poke, they thot it was life, so trapped at the bottom of sunless holes, they crawled on each other and ate garbage. Death was worshipped and passed on as a ritual of grace.

chaka doo chaka doo chakadoo chakadoo the
rite

> the might of the spirit
> the rise of the sun men
> through love and creation
> they called it a nation.

It was a new man they build. It was a new life, a new path, for all everyone who had the rhythm of vision

> who sucked on bones
> they beat them chakadoo chaka chaka chaka
> chaka chaka

they beat them and played them
something slow as a mineral is a vehicle for
        God
the use
is the soul touch
the connector with all
yr clothes is a nose in clean air
yr eyes see light the prince grows ka ka ka ka
        ka
the image of prince black prince black brother
        black father
ka ka ka ka ka ka ka
the soul of the nation ba ba ba ba ba
the mighty sun nation
ra, the sun, ra, the sun,
all the universe changes
and what does not change, is inexpressible

ED BULLINS

Seventh Avenue Poem

(*to Billy*)

. . . and I walked
into this
bar
& saw
Ad

      am

          clay

          ton
POWELL
with a glass

in one
hand
& a

L/ASS
in the
other

. . . and I walked
out
knowin'
I can't

stomach
long funerals

but Never
give up
on his
tory
I remember
to say

. . . and I THINK
I should'a
stopped
drinkin'
along
       time
ago

Spirit Enchantment

Open your ears to spirit sounds
Open your ears to secret words
Open your mind to spirit songs
Open your soul to receive
Spirits of your family
Spirits of your kind
Spirits of yourself
Sounds of the secret places
Songs of the invisible spaces
Come sing the warm songs sung
in the inner self
come sing the warm songs sung
in the inner self
come sing the warm songs sung
in the inner self
Oh . . . help me lawd . . .
sing the warm songs sung
in the inner self
in the inner self
in the inner self
yas . . . indeed . . .

STANLEY CROUCH

Pimp's Last Mack: Death RE quest.

A Folk Song

On the way to the bone orchard, the
dirt house of all the gone daddies' bones,
I want to go slump-sided—
on a dago, tilted over just a little.
I want 3 short fat greasy ho's in red on one side
& three creole queens 7 foot tall on the other side
lowering me in the ground from 7 gold chains.
But on the way I want my casket dragged by 13 giant snakes
                                                    painted riot ruby red
and on top of that gold and silver flip top cigar
I want a 3-headed purple nigguh baby
blowing 11 connected bugles full of burning nappy hair
and smearing the top with his muddy feet
and pissing in the tracks left by my coffin's dragging
and 6 devils' feet behind
I want a crowd of blue-eyed baboons sucking the yellow out
                                                    of those lines
my casket be leaving on the way to the bone
orchard, dirt house of all the gone daddies' bones.
WAIT!
And in the   l a s t   of the long road go down
amongst the epitaphs & trees—
wooden ropes holding the grass down—
I want MY grave note to say in gold AND silver:

To dirt, sin, low life
and fast women of river hips

who baptized him nightly
this young man was no stranger.
And when he sat his black ass down
his butt hole stamped down
            DANGER!

Albert Ayler: Eulogy
for a decomposed saxophone player

(The saxophone turned into a dolphin
or a flying shark with transparent teeth of fire
behind which the shadows of ghosts could be seen dancing
or a seal spinning sound under the ice
you wore a leather suit
and the metal pipe covered with stemmed buttons
plucked the notes off the music and left the sound.
Don felt fresh wind in his face
Don Cherry did at first hearing you
when we wind back to scandanavia
and the legends begin)

1. GHOSTS (the national anthem)

Sometimes a saxophone
is a home
twisting dead women
through the air
(You feel the hymn
the old lonely hymn
the hymn we all never would've sung)

2. SPIRITS REJOICE

And we can step high
And we can step high

and we can high step
and walk away

And we can step high and we can step high and we can high
    step and walk away

Don't you know that the old black men
now walk across the fields
walking slowly up their deaths

But don't you know that the old black men's
souls shout *high* across the fields

3. EAST RIVER REFLECTION

But we could never rejoice in the river
only decompose in the dark
the flesh-ringing dumplings in the water of november.
Did the east river bite your heart,
did it bite, Albert,
while exhibitionists,
flipping themselves out,
waved from bridges?
Did the water, that wet cold fist with slobbering ripples for
    lines of a palm,
did the water make your body look as much like a
sea horse as your saxophone looked like one—
but you though in the scales and stretches of decomposition
Mr. Albert Ayler

the old men's marcher
twisting the voices of dead women through the air
and it is the river
puzzleboard pieces of ice
and no more gray flames of drummer's howls
in the blue background

4. BELLS

      We walk
      We hum
we summon streets
we shout down the streets
we moan down the streets
we kick spit curse and sing

It is never warm now
No days

5. LAST STAND (as the flesh rises & waves away)

And the sharp nails of our notes
become burry picks with which we climb mountains.
Up that mountain of horizontal rungs of air
the chest has to be big to sing any song way up that high—
      up *there:*
the atmosphere thin with ghosts
weaving through saxophones

and we'll remember, Albert,
as we walk, as we hum,
that you sang up there, playing
the bells—summoning—in a ferocious, a growling,
a honking big-heartedness
before the air was greased
up under the bottom of your feet
and you fell, were pushed, accepting "the river's invitation"
and the water plucked your beard
with it filth and its cans, its garbage,
plucked your beard,
and your flesh
now a slimy brown harpsichord slapped ashore
November 25, 1970.

RONDA DAVIS

I Am Here to Announce

*. . . . . in honor of Malcolm, who was called
by Carolyn (Rodgers) "the Mightiest cleanser."*

i am here to announce
that i am *not* a poet
not of the usual kind, that is

that is
the kind who reads *poems*
beats out to you the sound of the words from the paper
through an instrument we know as voice

that is
the kind who sits up and scratches out words
(on the paper)
and hands your or reads you the finished product
                              honed
                              honeyed up
                              made right/uptight/
                                   toog*eh*ther

the kind who
uses erasers and stufflikethat

the kind of poet who WRITES kind truths
                         in beautiful ways
                         unkind truths
                         in meaningful ways

whose fingers some spirit speaks through
writes through.
i am here to announce
that i am *not* that kind of poet:
color me poem.
color me rough
color me raggedy
color me unready
color me an un-finished poem
that is,
the kind of poem you say there's hope for
there's room for improvement in
there's a few good lines in
a few catchy phrases in
color me the kind of poem that just needs
a little work.
a good beginning—
maybe just in need of a punch line.

part two:

a poet—one who poze it out
.color me unpoed.
a poem—something that flows freely
.color me stuck.
been holdin own to nice things to say to nice peepo
been holdin own to eevo things to say to eevo peepo
been so long waitin fuh thuh *right* time

[49]

been spendin time watchin time
been holdin own

aint been flowin
aint been gettin toothuhbottomuh things

a poet:
God's, Allah's, the Creator's
Is the Chief Gardener's fruit
of the tree
that earth is.
poet is produce.   like: cola nut
             apple
             orange
             apple
             .an apple.
             yeah.
             we back in Eden now and
                you can
color me the problem. an apple. rotten-to-the-core.
color me new york
flavored ice cream is SO much sweeter than i am

i am (h)ome in
chicago
flavored ice cream and
    i scream at you that
    i am here today
    in three layers
    ALL sweeter than

       i really am:
—chicago ice cream is orange sherbet and
  i am sure bit by some i-hate-me-bug

—chicago ice cream is vanilla and
  i am still a little bit white inside
  the enemy is stilla inna me

—chicago ice cream is coffee and
  i KNOW
  i am chicago
  cause coffee is always grounds for change.

      i scream hurt all over with a chocolate icing
      i am frozen from love
      and-don't-you-touch-me-cause-i-will-stick-to-you

color me a chicago poem because i scream all over in three
significant layers of hurt.

i am ill.
color me chicago *ill* i *noise* poem.

part three:

i am here to announce
that i *am* the poem
and sometimes
because i am the absence of myself
i am the absence of poetry

[51]

i ask that you correct me—if i'm wrong
i seem to have forgotten my pen
and how to use it
to correct myself

i have forgotten
how to read *me*
seem to be afraid
of the handwriting on the wall

color me wall-tear
and
tear me down, somebody
and build me up, somesoul

part four:

i stand here WORDS before you
a group of words called ronda
a world of words hanging all around me
screaming:
"spress yoself
spell yoself out
put som poetry in this one verse of a universe
hey, word, ronda,
you are one of those things that makes the world go round
spinnnnn!
put a spell on you—deep magic possibility playing possum
correct yoself
or you will die as you live

and you will never know what your word means
    you will never know what you sound like
    in this earth that is ears
    you will never know that you ARE the sound of the ears
print yoself, child
write yoself out and up, honey
                hone   up
                and   you   own up
                to   yo   own thing
                do it   now
                do it   now
                do it   now
                do it   now
                don't just make do. do it.
                            do do
                            do do
                            do do
                            do dodo shit
is the "name of the game"
i stand here before you a group of words spelled shit

part five:

and i am so proud to be shit. it
is the first step in cleansing.

when you toilet—toil it—toil at it
when you work it out
when you do yo thang thang
you just about a sonofa john.

[53]

part six:

take this son/me home with you
ahma sun again shining daughter of my mother and father
i am a child again
in need of a wipe
        a flush
        a rinse
        baptize me
and make my thoughts smell like love again
be John for this son, my peepo. peep the me in you, godians.
it's johnson time
and i'm callin on YOU
a nation of johnitors
to shine-on ME
BE: "johnson, the first cweam winse for childwen"
tired of getting stuck in the tangles of me
spray me with some LOVE
and i will be your microphone
and play you back
the sound of your love
times ten

part seven:

i am here to announce
that i/we am a poem

                in need of righting
                in need of standing up

                        in need of getting the kinks out
                        so the master's piece can show
i am here to announce
that i will lay ME down for the righting
i ask that you do not step on me
while i am john searching for the ronda
                    searching for the ra and the da
                    searching for the light and the giving
                    searching for the shine in me

i am here to announce
that i respond well to art gum erasers
and other soft touch cleaners
made to clear up
and not rub out

i am here to announce
that clean-up week
is the next national holiday
for a national of peepo
that i KNOW
i am NOT that different from.

Debra: An Africanese Name Reading
On the Sound of Debra

Debra
u are like de-*BRA*
deb-bra-a supporter of so many
sizes shapes and forms of ideas
u are,
debra.

u are a LARGE soul
can be branded a playTexan
cause
they grow um big in debraland too.
sister—you are a monument to the sun
    when   you are all
    that   you are.
playTexan
you so close to Arizona,
Phoenix Bird,
I can already see your wings reshaping.
Debra is a rising zone.

Debra,
I know you dream of yourself in many situations—

a maiden's form of let-me-be-free ideas
some of which may
one day
fly us all home to ourselves.
keep your dreams/your points of view.
a righteous dream for yourself, debby,
IS a dream for your people.

Debra.   de BRA: brace yourself for job preparation.
                     YOU ARE HERE TO SUPPORT SOULS.

                     You must learn to pull
                     to pull your own covers off—first.
                     de-bra, debra
                     take it ALL off, and reknow yourself.

2.

Debra is uh D thang.
and
Deebruh is for *DI*ETY, God-creature, Lady Dee.
Dee it, Dee
Be Dee, Dee
Be Dee, Diety
Don't be DeeDangerous
     be TeeTerrible-lee BAD
     cause that's good.

3.

Debby.
Deh-BEE.
Debby is uh B thang, too.
sting self, Bee,
then turn on us
Bzzzzzzzzzzzzzzzz but AW!wayz remember
to hurt righteously.

Debbies are Be-ers:
Be uh miller - uh fixit person.
             uh maker of your U

Say to yourself: "I can work it out
     I can be stevedore digging into
      the wonder(full)ness
    of myself."
Grind at the soil of you, Debby Miller,
There are ancient treasures there.
Reach down
Reach deep
Reach out
Reach UP to Beeing the next best thing
to love.
then
Be love, be-er.
U are not alone in the search.

    4.

Debrah. Deb-RA.
Be the Ra in yourself.
Be stone Ra
 stone rock
Dis-cover
the sun in your core,
sun goddess.
It's Egypt-trip-time
in the eyes of
a Deb-RA. a deb named RA.
gonna

have uh comin out party
gonna
all come out and support
The Egyptian Deb: WHILE she becomes RA
                    WHEN   she becomes RA
        because she MUST   become RA
gonna
RA RA you ohn, Debby
        you ohn
        you own the world
now TOP it
   SCOPE it, debutant
                deb, u tanto
                    u got uh long range to cover.
   DO UH DEBRA THING!
deb, be uh RA
deb, be RA
Debby RA
Debby RA
Debby-RA. Debra . . . . . Bzzzzzzzzzzz Debra!

JACKIE EARLEY

The Gospel Truth

Is that
The Blacman can not be destroyed.
I sed
The Blacman can not be destroyed.

He has a Force, a Spirit honey
That can not be killed. He has
A Force, Energy, and Mission
To be/the Creator.

Who else could be a blacman?
Be branded a savage
Be stolen from your home
Be chained
Be broken down, destroyed
'N sold into slavery.
Be raped, castrated,
Prostituted and brainwashed . . .
Then go be lynched.

Tricked into separation
Poisoned with pig, and wine and dope . . .
And in spite of all that . . .
Survive/to sing the blues.
Survive/to holler in some cotton field
Jump Jesus! Shout for joy.
Go get clean on Setday night.
Get you hair did.

Carry your dead in some cadilacs.
Create a language that moves a country
'N a rythm that won't let 'em quit.

Then be the world's fastest runner—
The world's greatest fighter—
Keep, you some money
And cities full of kids.
Run up against a Sherman tank
With just an 'ole empty bottle;
Survive all of that
'N give birth to a daughter
Who creates poetry
About what you been thru.

That is when you will know for yourself
That/the Blacman can not be destroyed.
He has a Force, a Spirit honey
That/can not be killed.

#2

The Gospel Truth
Is that
The Blacwoman can not be destroyed.
I sed
The Blacwoman can not be destroyed.

She has a Force, a Spirit honey
That can not be killed. She has

A Force, Energy, and Mission
To be/the Creator.

Who else could be a Blackwoman?
Full of amazing grace!
With the face of eternity,
Queen of the Human Race.
Who gets sold into slavery
Crushed, clothes torn
Raped, yet refuse to mourn?
Be calling for your man
And be looking for your son.
Be greeted with a face of white
Be beat and stripped, then sold.
Have your fetus robbed each year.
Watch your mutilated baby die
Yet sing some cracker's "lullaby."

Be worked worse than your man.
Watch him beaten, see him cry.
Know/that he disappeared one night;
Yet/send your kids to school on time.
Keep all of them alive.
Survive to be a grandmother.
Build a church before you die.
Leave a gleam in some man's eyes
That creates a daughter who poets
Who writes glory in the sky!
Just for you to understand
Why/the BlacOnes will survive.
And that's/the Gospel Truth.

One Thousand Nine- Hundred & Sixty- Eight Winters . . .

> Got up this morning
> Feeling good & Black
> Thinking black thoughts
> Did black things
> Played all my black records
> And minded my own black bidness!
>
> Put on my best black clothes
> Walked out my black door
> And . . .
>
> Lord have Mercy!
> *White*
> Snow!

MARI EVANS

Where Have You Gone

Where have you gone

with your confident
walk with
your crooked smile

why did you leave
me
when you took your
laughter
and departed

are you aware that
with you
went the sun
all light
and what few stars
there were?

where have you gone
with your confident

walk your
crooked smile the
rent money
in one pocket and
my heart
in another .   .   .

a good assassination
should be quiet

                      he had
                      A Dream
        e   x   p   loded
                down
                      his
                         th   r   o   a   t.

            whereon
    a million hard white eyes
    swung impiously heavenward
            to mourn
    the gross indelicate demise

                      Such public death
                      transgresses
                      all known rules

            A good assassination
            should be quiet

            and occupy the heart
          four hundred
        years

[70]

princeling

> *swing sweet rhythm*
>> charcoal toes
> *swing sweet rhythm*
>> blooddripped knees
> *swing sweet rhythm*
>> exorcised penis
> *swing sweet rhythm*
>> My God—my son!

Brother. . . the twilight

brother . . .
The twilight of your loins
an eerie white encroaching
on your black fire
coldcircling all your beauty
your black strength
Mingle your warm love with mine
and with our last hands fling
the sweet black shit of our resistance
at the whitefaced
ovens . . .

NIKKI GIOVANNI

Poem of Angela Yvonne Davis

*i wrote this poem because i feel there are very few
flowers in this field we so dishonestly call life. and
so few are involved with living but my vibrations
from this woman, angela yvonne davis, are that she
wishes to live and that desire forced her involvement
to the point of death. and i listened to roberta flack
sing donny hathaway as he's never been sung saying
"you were mine for only a minute" with all the pain
of understanding the minute. and this woman
brought out feelings of hope for us that no one has
brought to me since i lost someone whom i love
more than . . . how can i say life when i have
continued to live though he too is gone.*

*they are all only ours for a very very brief time though
if we move in tune to time and space we will become
a part of them—matter being neither created nor
destroyable. and i watched the death of jimi hen-
dricks and people trying to say "he was not murdered" and i watched the death of a. d. king and
people trying to say "he was not murdered" and i am
watching my own death and the people saying "it is
an accident" and it is, though the accident is not my
death but my life and there are too many of us who
feel this way and not enough who can do what surely*

must be done. our feeling is used against us all the time and our feeling is what we must maintain. is there no way out of this quandry?

and i think angela yvonne has a love affair with life and she has given herself to that lover so completely that she must be consumed by her. and i thought if i talked with angela yvonne in tones other than the spirits or maybe if i tried to press her spirit between these characters from my typewriter and this paper what would it feel like. i offer in love this poem of angela yvonne davis, spoken as i think she would speak, because she's the other third of me—and some part of you.

i move on feeling and have learned to distrust those who
don't
i move in time and space determined by time and space
feeling
that all is natural and i am
a part of it and "how could you?" they ask you had everything
but the men who killed the children in birmingham aren't on
the most wanted list and the men who killed schwerner,
chaney
and goodman aren't on the most wanted list and the list of
names
unlisted could and probably would include most of our "finest

leaders" who are wanted in my estimation for at least serious
questioning so we made a list and listed it

"but you had everything." they said and i asked "quakers?"
                                                  and i asked
"jews?" and i asked "being sent from home?" my mother
                                     told me the world
would one day speak my name then she recently suggested
                                          angela yvonne
why don't you take up sports like your brother and i said "i
                                     don't run
as well as he" but they told me over and over again "you can
                                     have them
all at your feet" though i knew they were at my feet when i
                                     was born
and the heavens opened up sending the same streak of
                                     lightning through
my mother as through new york when i was arrested

and i saw my sisters and brothers and i heard them tell the
                                          young
racists "you can't march with us" and i thought i can't march
                                          at all
and i looked at the woman whose face was kissed by night
                                     as she said
"angela you shall be free" and i thought i won't be free even
                                     if i'm set
loose. the game is set the tragedy written my part is captive
i thought of betty shabazz and the voices who must have
                                     said "aren't you

sort of glad its over?" with that stupidity that fails to notice
it will never be over for some of us and our children and our
grandchildren. betty can no more forget that staccato than i
the pain
in jonathan's face or the love in george's letters. and i
remember
the letter where i asked "why don't you write beverly
axelrod and become
rich and famous" and his complete reply

i remember water and sky and paris and wanting someone
to be mine
a german? but the world is in love with germans so why not?
though
i being the youngest daughter of africa and the sun was
rejected
and all the while them saying "isn't she beautiful?" and she
being i
thinking "aren't you sick" and i remember wanting to give
myself but
nothing being big enough to take me and searching for the
right way
to live and seeing the answer understanding the right way to
die
though death is as distasteful as the second cigarette in the
morning
and don't you understand? i value my life so surely all others
must value
theirs and that's the weakness the weak use against us. they
so casually make decisions like who's going to live and who's
going to

starve to death and who will be happy or not and they never
know
what their life means since theirs lacks meaning and they
never
have to try to understand what some else's life could mean
those guards and policemen who so casually take the only
possession
worth possessing and dispense with it like an empty r.c. cola
bottle
never understanding the vitality of its contents

and the white boys and girls came with their little erections
and i
learned to see but not show feeling and i learned to talk
while not
screaming though i would scream if anyone understands
that language
and i would reach if there were a substance and Black
people say
i went communist and i only and always thought i went and
Black people
say "why howard johnson's" but i could think of no other
place and Black
people ask 'why didn't you shoot it out?' when i thought i
had. and they say
they have no responsibility and i knew they would not rest
until my
body was bought out in tiny flabby pieces

the list is long and our basic christianity teaches us to
sacrifice

the good to the evil and if the blood is type O positive maybe
they
will be satisfied but white people are like any other gods an
insatiatable
appetite and as long as we sacrifice our delicate to their
course we will sacrifice
i mean i started with a clear head cause i felt i should and
feeling
is much more than mere emotion though that is not to be
sacrificed
and through it all i was looking for this woman angela
yvonne

and i wanted to be harriet tubman who was the first
WANTED Black woman
and i wanted to bring myself and us out of the fear and into
the Dark
but my helpers trapped me and this i have learned of love—
it is harder
to be loved than to love and the responsibilities of letting
yourself
be loved are too great and perhaps i shall never love again
cause i would rather need than allow, and what i'm saying
is
i had five hours of freedom when i recognized my lovers
had decided
and i was free in my mind to say—whatever you do you
will not know

what you have done

we walked that october afternoon among the lights and
                              smells of autumn
people and i tried so to hold on. and as i turned 51st street
                              and eighth
and saw, i knew there was nothing more to say so i thought
and i entered the elevator touching the insides as a woman
                              is touched
i looked into the carpet as we were expelled
and entered the key
which would both open and close me
and i thought to them all
to myself just make it easy
on yourself

october 16, 1970

DAVID HENDERSON

Walk with the Mayor of Harlem

enter harlem
to walk from the howling cave
called the "A" train/
from columbus circle
                    (find america discovered)
all along a 66 block artillery blitz
                              to the quarter/
        non-stop
    existential TWA nightcoach
rome-to-auschwitz express
where multitudes vomit   pass out
witness death by many stabbings
upon pompei/
                please close the doors please
before the approach to the madness of washington heights
        disembark   /silent moot   of black vectors
to sunder this quarter
                        thru

black mass
black land

of rhythm n
            blues & the fish of jesus
snake dancers walk mojo along wide boulevards
sight for those
            who live away

a new land!
no dream stuff
    in dem black neon clouds of de full moon
                to illume by sun-ra
streets just like you
               no thinking you crazy
vertigo
    under skyscrapers/

        II

where harlem lies
        find no industrial green
                  giants
only
    bojangling children in the streets
only
    the sleeping car brotherhood of underground males
only
    the knights of the mystic sea
find only
      the black sapphires
      of the beulah baptist methodist church on the
                     mount
here
    clustered & cross-purposed
some people say
ebony is an imitation of life
           you take it where you find it
           or you can leave it like it is

talk to me   talk to me
talk to me   talk to me
                tell me like it is
the memory   of sky watch
sun dance   drum chant   body-ruba
sharp are the signals thru the skin
thru bones
hard as the forgotten legions
of
the giant bushmen

O beulah baptist in the streets/
to the paradise songs of bloodletting
the gospel singers   are   asayin/
the world is in a troubled time
when
        the knights of the mystic sea
clash
        with the sicilian asphalt paving company
a blood ruckus
        will ensue
that night
there will be moonsoon rains over harlem
helicopters colliding with tenements
               in orange suprise
night letters to newark
        /For LeRoi

Hanging Out in the Music
Poem 1

he breathed the hot room alive with jass and vivid colors.
breathed in and out. faces raptured towards the light made by
jass playing towards the light. brilliant. faces facing

he felt sparks of energy along his back, the wingspread
                                                    within
without. his eyes opened wider, he saw everything in the
                                                    room
at once. and there was so much. the trumpet hit a trill. a bad
hatchet. his stomach fluttered.

he sat up upon his stomach. the seat of wind. he felt the
                                                    energy
possessed by the electric winds within his sac. the seat of
                                                    wind.
the power to digest, to breakdown. the energy of atoms.

then. sensitized to open the eyes. a tickling occurring. twinkle
of brilliance in the room. high yellows and cosmic shango
                                                    red
. . . a fireness.

sensitized. like a kiss upon the eyes. tender lips brushing.
enhance consciousness of respiration. of acoming in and out.
with life and the death is exhaled. enhance the respiration.
deepen the ears to the room containing all.

jass they play. you hear at it. it be a part of you. alive
it be alive. like when you alone in the house. maybe a little
lonely. you put on some bad jass. and they be company.

you hear they grow. you see them play. the musicians. they
be
going thru changes. just in the music. like you be going thru
changes like the jass. tunes.

4th Dimension

in order to do. he sat in his room at nights and asked the
      moon.
the moon led him from his window into the night. steam
      rose in the
white light. the night was wet. the moon wore a ring of fire.
      he
walked he knew not where until he came to a store front. he
      stopped.

in to the night. her tongue came out of her face lit by a dim
amber light. she glowed as if her blood were warm and blue.
she came close so he smelled her breath flushed in short
      panting
breaths straight whiskey sweet methedrine   her tongue was
      extremely wet.
it washed across his eyes and stuck in his nose.

a softness of cloths. rustling blue. like delicate drapes in a
      night breeze.
he put his face through it all. it plunged into mounds and
      hills
of a lived softness, and then he felt what made him at once
      hungry. the smell
of the inside of a body. interior strange odor. like the smell
      of hashish
in the air only something that does not burn but is alive.

the exhausts of the bus became the taste of bourbon. the
       sun was bombing
the apartment buildings.

the port wine the bowery dudes drank was very good for
       giving one
the state of departure from the body. a disembodied stagger
       thru
afternoon streets that looked like cartoon. a softness of body
       could
be dashed to the ground and not feel it. you wake up in the
       middle of
the night screaming. you stop. you laugh and go back to
       sleep.

MAE JACKSON

Please

The rap continues with the bad dude in the lead
their faces covering the "national magazines"
looking mean
talking rapidly and inconsistently
trying to be logical about revolution?

The rap continues
as offers from hollywood pour in by the thousands
WANTED WANTED
BAD NIGGER ACTORS
OR BAD ACTING NIGGERS
FOR T.V. AND HOLLYWOODSTYLEDREVOLUTION
mean while
            (back in the ghetto)
the vanguard prepares a press statement
announcing that they are going underground
and the real revolutionary
richard milhouse nixon
puts his program into action: "genocide"

WANTED WANTED
NEED TO BE DONE NOW
WILL   THE   REAL   WARRIORS   PLEASE   KEEP   YOUR
        MOUTH CLOSED

Poems for the Lonely

1.

i
here
within myself
centuries of self hate
that know no way to destruct
that know no way
to break loose
chained to myself
as i stand
and watch me die
i slowly protest the death of others

2.

what better way to say goodbye
than this
to toast your young dream
my cup runneth over

what better way to leave
than to leave you this way

what better way to say that i understand
than this
as i say goodbye
i
leave

NORMAN JORDAN

Popsicle Cold

Now
that the story
has moved
out of the headlines
the widow
of the dead black hero
stands alone
at the public market
purchasing polluted pork
with government
food stamps.

Brothers the Struggle Must Go On

(*Members don't git weary*)

Despite
the strange noises
from the empty
apartment next door
(or the open-mouthed
winehead corpse
at the end
of the hall)

We must
lay the
evidence
on the table

and forget
the outline
of the door
that appears
in our heads
when we first
close our eyes.

Clairvoyance

City birds
fly in small bunches
on Sunday morning
as if they knew
what happened
the night before.

Mind and Soul After Dark

Naked
Scalding Wet
from the Sea
My soul stands Wobbly
on its hind legs
the ghost of an exhausted Poet
My mind returning from the brink of surrender
reaches out
for a formal position
together
shaking the dust of a thousand deaths
returning from a mad dream
together
desperately trying to grasp and
observe the last days of Spring.

GYLAN KAIN

Song of Ditta

PART II

Wah-hoo
Mama tits
pluck me when its over
my mind is a dying hawk
ash and the asses
ash and the asses
and the curling toe
beneath the gutter
ain't nothing happening but
pigs and poets
cause they both wallow in the earth
Fly me to the moon was a cracker's dream
But Icarius died beneath the sun on wings of steel
We call ourselves the Black-white men
While Tonto spoke with a pitched fork tongue
Song of Solomom
Black and comely
Ah, but the airplanes sits on the breasts of my dream
The Trojan Horse
and the burden
take it out
The 19th century-sleeping clocks
and the Spaniard
The image smears
against the soft white lie
"Shall I pick my nose
or scratch my ass"

Said the clairol lady
as she swayed in the casket winds
winds
The windmills and the foolish knight
Rosinante/a fallen horse
mainline sucking on a nightmare
We are so many fireflies that dash against the wall
and then pretend that God is dead
Lords of the flies
The fantasy
The reality
The burning sorrow
and the wind
Open your legs
What shall I say
Holy Mary mother of god—
question mark
We live out our lives on motorcycles
wedged between the cubbyhole
of death and the confessing priest
Dogs fly
collars turn round
In the illusory world/promises
with its lips against the window
Promises
     with its lips against the window
Promises
     Pigs and machine guns
and your daughter dying in the corner
with tears that mop the floor

She licks the wound
    with tears that mop the floor
and the pig in the window
    fear not
God was an only child
and jealousy was a whore
Mama lifted her bosoms
And the stars sang songs of Hosanna
I am not the fool
you bargained for
Nor am I the open desert
or the rats
that patrol the sewers
I am your mirrors image
After the volcanic mist
I am the water rising
and the buzzard
and the lost desert
of the 5 dicks lie rotting
Erection has no father

          Amen

KALI

Black Is

Black is something to laugh about
Black is something to cry about
Black is serious
Black is a feeling
Black is us the beautiful people

Circles

ONCE UPON A TIME THERE WERE THREE BLACK LINES, NOW ONE LINE HAD A WHITE CIRCLE AND THE OTHER HAD A BLACK CIRCLE AND THE LAST ONE HAD A YELLOW CIRCLE. NOW THE WHITE CIRCLE HAD HER EYE ON THE YELLOW CIRCLE'S MAN. SO ONE DAY THE WHITE CIRCLE JAMMED THE YELLOW CIRCLE AGAINST THE TRIANGLE AND SAID I HAVE A KNIFE IN MY POCKET WE WILL TRADE MEN NOW THE WHITE CIRCLE HAD THE OTHER BLACK LINE SOON THE YELLOW CIRCLE WAS FIGHTING THE WHITE ONE. THE BLACK CIRCLE SAW THIS AND CHIPPED IN FOR THE YELLOW CIRCLE AND THE BLACK AND YELLOW CIRCLE WON. IT JUST GOES TO SHOW WHAT A LITTLE TEAM WORK CAN DO.

What's Happening to the Heroes

AUNT JEMIMA DEAD
MOTHER GOOSE IS DYING
THE LAW FOUND THE
TRUE AGE OF ROBIN
AND SAID HE WOULD HAVE
TO GO TO SCHOOL
AND ON THE WAY TO SCHOOL
THE BATMOBEL BROKE.
CLARK KENT CAN'T FLY
INTO SUPERMAN BECAUSE
SUPERMAN CAN'T FLY.
TONTO WENT BACK TO HIS
PEOPLE AND LONE RANGER IS
ALL ALONE
THAT'S WHAT'S HAPPENING

KEORAPETSE KGOSITSILE

Point of Departure

Fire Dance Fire Song

(A wise old man told me in Alabama;
"Yeah, Ah believes in nonviolence
alright. But de only way to say
nonviolen' in dis man's country is
to keep a gun an' use it." Four
years earlier another wise old man
had told me the same thing near
Pietersburg in South Africa. He
said his words of wisdom is Sepedi.)

I. THE ELEGANCE OF MEMORY

Distances separate bodies not people. Ask
Those who have known sadness or joy
The bone of feeling is pried open
By a song, the elegance
Of color a familiar smell, this
Flower or the approach of an evening . . .

All this is NOW

I used to wonder
Was her grave warm enough,
'Madikeledi, my grandmother,
As big-spirited as she was big-legged,
She would talk to me. She would . . .
How could I know her sadness then
Or who broke my father's back?
But now . . .

The elegance of memory,
Deeper than the grave
Where she went before I could
Know her sadness, is larger
Than the distance between
My country and I. Things more solid
Than the rocks with which those sinister
Thieves tried to break our back

I hear her now. And I wonder
Now does she know the strength of the fabric
She wove in my heart for us? . . . Her
Voice clearer now than then: Boykie,
Dont ever take any nonsense from *them,*
You hear!

                There are memories between us
Deeper than grief. There are
Feelings between us much stronger
Than the cold enemy machine that breaks
The back. Sister, there are places between us
Deeper than the ocean, no distances.
Pry your heart open, brother, mine too,
Learn to love the clear voice
The music in the memory pried
Open to the bone of feeling, no distances

II. LUMUMBA SECTION

Searching past what we see and hear
Seering past the pretensions of knowledge
We move to the meeting place,
The pulse of the beginning the end and the beginning
In the stillnesses of the night
We see the gaping wounds where
Those murderers butchered your flesh
As they butchered the flesh of our land
Spirit to spirit we hear you
Then blood on blood comes the pledge
Swift as image, in spirit and blood
The sons and daughters of our beginnings
Boldly move to post-white fearlessness
Their sharpnesses at the murderer's throat
Carving your song on the face of the earth
In the stillnesses of the night
Informed by the rhythm of your spirit
We hear the song of warriors
And rejoice to find fire in our hands
"Aint no mountain high enough . . ." Dig it,
The silences of the wind know it too
"Aint no valley low enough . . ."
Freedom, how do you do!

III. FIRE DANCE

There will be no dreaming about escape
There will be no bullshit coldwar talk
    The fire burns to re-create
    the rhythms of our timeless acts
    This fire burns timeless in our
    time to destroy all nigger chains
    as real men and women emerge
    from the ruins of the rape by white greed

    The rape by savages who want to control
    us, memory, nature. Savages who even forge
    measures to try to control time. Dont you
    know time is not a succession of hours!
    Time is always NOW, dont you know!
    Listen to the drums. That there is a point of departure
    NOW is always the time. Praise be to Charlie Parker
    And it dont have nothing to do with hours

Now sing a song of NOW
A song of the union of pastandfuture
Sing a song of blood—The African miner, his body
Clattering to the ground with mine phthisis:
That there is murder. Do the dance of fire
The rhythm of young black men
Burning these evil white maniacs

My Name Is Afrika

(*for ngabeni mthimkhulu*)

All things come to pass
When they do, if they do
All things come to their end
When they do, as they do
So will the day of the stench of oppression
Leaving nothing but the lingering
Taste of particles of hatred
Woven around the tropical sun
While in the belly of the night
Drums roll and peal a monumental song . . .
To every birth its blood
All things come to pass
When they do
We are the gods of our day and us
Panthers with claws of fire
And songs of love for the newly born
There will be ruins in Zimbabwe for real
Didn't Rap say,
They used to call it Detroit
And now they call it Destroyed!
To every birth its pain
All else is death or life

DON L. LEE

But He Was Cool
or: he even stopped for green lights

super-cool
ultrablack
a tan/purple
had a beautiful shade.

he had a double-natural
that wd put the sisters to shame.
his dashikis were tailor made
& his beads were imported sea shells
    (from some blk/country i never heard of)
he was triple-hip

his tikis were hand carved
out of ivory
& came express from the motherland.
he would greet u in swahili
& say good-by in yoruba.
wooooooooooooo-jim he bes so cool & ill tel li gent
                cool-cool is so cool he was un-cooled by
                   other niggers' cool
                cool-cool ultracool was bop-cool/ice box
                  cool so cool cold cool

his wine didn't have to be cooled, him was
air conditioned cool
cool-cool/real cool made me cool—now
ain't that cool
cool-cool so cool him nick-named refrig-
erator.

cool-cool so cool
he didn't know,
after detroit, newark, chicago &c.,
we had to hip
cool-cool/super-cool/real cool
that
to be black
is
to be
very-hot.

Blackwoman

blackwoman:
is an
in and out
rightsideup
action-image
of her man . . . .
in other
(blacker) words;
she's together,
if
he
bes.

A Poem Looking for a Reader

(to be read with a love consciousness)

black is not
all inclusive,
there are other colors.
color her warm and womanly,
color her feeling and life,
color her a gibran poem & 4 women of simone.
children will give her color
paint her the color of her
man.

most of all color her
love
a remembrance of life
a truereflection
that we
will
move   u will move with
i want
u
a fifty minute call to blackwomanworld :
                    hi baby,
                    how u doin?
need u.
listening to
young-holt's, *please sunshine, please.*

[117]

to give   i'll give
most personal.
what about the other
scenes: children playing in vacant lots,
            or like the first time u knowingly kissed a girl,
            was it joy or just beautifully beautiful.

i
remember at 13
reading chester himes'
cast the first stone and
the eyes of momma when she caught me: read on, son.

how will u come:
            like a soulful strut in a two-piece beige o-rig'i-nal,
            or afro-down with a beat in yr/walk?
how will love come:
            painless and deep like a razor cut
            or like some cheap 75¢ movie;
            i think not.

will she be the woman
other men will want
or
will her beauty be
accented with my name on it?

she will come as she would
want her man to come.
she'll come,
she'll come.
i
never wrote a love letter
but
that doesn't mean
i
don't love.

FELIPE LUCIANO

You're Nothing But a Spanish Colored Kid

I see them
Puerto Ricans/Spanish niggers
Bronzed farmers look silly being doormen
Their fingers are more honest than their eyes.
Earth hands turned metallic gray
The plow rots, the mule dies, the hands rust
And the elders sit with ashes on their crowns
making fools of themselves in bars.
Those fingertips will never touch the soil again.
Those fingertips will never feel the fuzz of
small stones smoothed for centuries by the river.
Fingertips/a nigger's Mount Rushmore
Fingertips
Drunkenly wrapped around a beer can
Hatefully curled through a belt
Desperately clutching a needle
Lost their land/Losing their minds
The conga was smashed by a machine
It could always vibrate, but it couldn't move an inch.
Well, we never threatened the music teacher anyway.
Fingers frozen
No fire in the loins
Brown people look so funny in the snow.
Frostbite of the soul
Condemned to a metal existence
Rapidly becoming plastic
A little more warmth, a lot more deceptive.

The sighted blind ask where are the chains
And I run lest they hang me for showing them the cross.
Porto Ricans/Indo Afros
Grasping for the good and dinding rusty machetes
Dangling from the thighs of their mothers
Waiting
Como se dice, Domino cho-cho
How do you say that chico?
Pelea, pelea, pelea
Talk that mira-mira shit now, Chico
Say it now, I'm Rican and proud
'Cause your years are numbered and daylight lasts
But so long.
Lose your color if you want to.
Me? I'm a war counselor for the the Sun
From a powder puff to jitterbugging with a star.
Beware the power of chisels made of powder puffs
They're like jealous lovers
Who slash silently regardless of who started the affair.
C'mon spic.
Learn to tell time.
Your daddy was a peasant
And you're nothing but a Spanish colored kid
unless you
Get real nigger
And stop making gestures.

Hot Blood/Bad Blood

Hot blood/Bad blood
You a machete and a pyramid
A nigger gone wild
An Indian madman and a Congo rhythm
Uh,Uh,Uh
You a bleeding horn in April
And a sweat-glistened locomotive in July
You a juju iceman and a steam tipped prayer
You a conga and a chant
A frosty kind of heat that sears a frown on your soul
Flip your eyeballs backward/inward
Can you see yourself?
You a conga and a bomba
and a plena and a chant
And a mambo number eight
Cause the seven others are sacred
Do you see yourself now?
Dreamlike almost, the rhythms/your pulse
Moving me, you like a muted trumpet on a
foggy, damp day in Harlem
Do you see the colors?
Do you see the colors of
walking blue, strutting violet
knife-wielding red and Christian grey?
Do you feel the moistness of that yellow hue
on your nipple/the weight of centuries of

blue-black on your thighs/the pressure of
white black on your temples?
Hot blood/Bad blood
I implore you by day to make love to me.
And by night I stick holes in the covering
of my womb
Make me pregnant with your hopes
so that I might give birth to words,
bullets, notes, and screams.
A barren artist is a starving lizard
is a barren artist is a shame.
Hot blood/Bad blood
From a lyrical seed-thrower
to an eight cylinder poem
From a mask carver when you feel high
to a face carver when you feel low.
Hi-low and the eight ball is us again
C'mere stuff
We, the sometimes artists, salute you
the everyday people.

CLARENCE MAJOR

Instant Revolution

so you dig instant revolution. how about
rotten meat. nauseous mariners, black spirits
move along as disobedient ancient sailors
in an urban ship of our lineal

navy, through the metal of white fog.   sniff
the odor of death as we pick up
speed across the pump   extravagance of our
                    enormous enemy.
who still, (a religious extremist, shy bitch & a perfumed
                    puritan) try to cram
our need with the scuffy variety of his garbage,
the flesh, the thick worms white, wiggle. A trick
whipped on us: like I saw these russian sailors, circa
1917 in a yellowed nontalking film upagainst the same
bullshit. who took over the ship and
cut the oppressor up into little pieces, a

view unexpected, and dropped   them down
with excruciating slow-
ness through the black ocean of Albert Ryder's bad eyesight.

And now again:

the spirit of those same fuckfaces move across concrete
tides viscious though soft, with soft undersides, soft eyes
killing   our brilliant darkness, splitting our

natural conflict! our natural beauty (of self & state

while my ancient brains/eyes
cruise the Hollywood version of their history, the gulf
of our salty spirits, taste and smell the technological future
(of us all
transmitted in his eye; while his women turn
against his conception screaming another fertilization
        another
pregnancy; yet you can measure his dull achievement by
the enamel of his skin. Measure his science in the dust
of his scriptures; know his errors (and our own
from the caves of his fetus to the nucleus of his moon landing.

And in terms of psychology. And in terms of sociology.
the spirit of our warships, tall narcotic, terrible structures
move along 63rd Street, drift the tide of 125th, as
across the atlantic, a
disposition (as all human dispositions
of navigated greed   but this time with a true moral: or

was it where I personally started, the environment
: a water fountain, *white only* in Texas
                    in Florida
                    in Georgia
                    in North Carolina
                    in Mississippi
my neck   cut by a rope of lust, turning me
to concrete, where my lungs no longer lungs. "Stop nigger

stop these bricks with your head in midair!" or

my corrosion in: creasing, as I pass their sunglass-
covered eyes arrogant in Mexico, these
institutions symbols, designed to operate against
the dark wisdom we know; so

down wind, like a mad hunter, I move. Against the
high peaks of technology, detecting the weak spots in
the cluster of his strength. Where he cannot pull
the loose ends together.

So weak in fact even blind desperate junkies shall lead
him to the edge of the earth and laugh when he, in his
sickness, thinking himself Rudolph Valentino, a great
lover in the black desert, jumps.

Widow

her room grows in her stale
building. Unable to fall. A whispy-bearded
                 old man tends the hedges,
outside. The policemen patrol the block;
she sees an empire from her window. She will
be fifty morning tomorrow. A decade
of brushfire crossfire. Character development.
The threat of juvenile delinquents. In
                 the heartbeat. Joints.
Hands and arms. Hormones. She makes speeches
at work and counts money. Lives in New York
and dreams of New Mexico. Her principles
are material. Menstruation menopause, past.
Glory ahead, Kingdom Green Pastures. God &
                 Christ characteristics.
Safe corners trappings at home & away. Her
rooms are four and her own spaces. She
                 sees better in age but
didn't expect the face in the mirror. Yet
it endures. Tho she herself in her mind,
                 changes in haste to youth
but with the comfort of growth

Being Different

i continued to walk backwards with no balance.
all of them now watching the slits in my example,
brave dude so generous, security meant laughter
inside rejected people, anymore voices coming out,
come *out* then!

all of their eyes on me hating me, aimless sense
so sudden and atrocious, pickling through my own
captions my brain, my subtitles, my muscles; yet
perspiring, my skin alive with fishhooks, my hands
open to rip the unyielding strangeness out
of what is beautiful!

AMUS MOR

Poem to the Hip Generation

(*Who are we? Where are we going? What are we here for?*)

david dug genesis
      did not dream
           heard the electric storm
               that was his intro
over the roof tops of grand blvd
      in the soup line's hey-day
           that lone wall of green
           and it must have been a kitchenette april's
              holy week
                with a man before him
          fetus to a nation's first step
            he was david

he was ageless on that birth
      with its strangle-hold on the infinite
8 lb Louis or lion
      on the welfare's tables
live a decade's spell
      until that day
anno domino decade
      and two years from explosion

the home runs on the grass
      set sail in a trunk
        when the rains came to the backs of the project
          units
        fred harris and the 12 kings blew gage in a open
          truck

and black nat sang of america majic boy
      so soon he was into the academy
of Lester the president

deeyoodaaadayodeedaadeedaaa
waayoobeeyoudaadooyoodeedaa
weyouudeeyoodaa

who are we
where are we going
what are we here for
      dadadoodaaleedaa
      datundoodadeedaa
not targets of the kelly boys
    with their twenty rifles
        snipers across may st
    two years from harry trumans great sin
    looking at the stone carvings on the buildings
under the ivy
        the wood lattices
    and the pidgeon stool on the window ledges
      we set men of tongues
and when they asked of us
    "will ford what are you doing in the lavatory this hour
    on my period"
      and we answered them
        "am smoking some shit"
      those tricks though we spoke of dung
      and so walked away saying
        "we'll have none of that kind of language
          here"

[135]

we coped and knew
        we slept brown and frizzly headed
      against the base of test tubes
and they scolded
        "what are you doing sleep in my classroom
        wake up ford or get out"
but we didn't care
         "cool" we answered
         and they thinking we spoke of the windows drafts
        walked away stiffly
    like the cinema monsters they almost were
        with their white smocks graying

we knocked the squares they were
        stood hip in their forum
         ran hip in their bungalowed streets
        wraped our girlfriends in our bears
      juiced and were warm
        in these basement bakers of 49
         we were always sister america
        beside you
         thats where i want to be
        i left my soullove in the river waiting for a helping
              hand
    we are the hip men
    we are here to conquer
    we are going to heaven
    and hell shall happen to states of their bodies

AS IT WAS IN THE BEGINNING

AS IT WAS IN THE BEGINNING AND EVEN SHALL BE WORLD
WITH END AMEN

    then pat was walking in that fine suede coat
that francis turned her onto
      laying in white bucks
        and a necks print scarf
and we heard who we really were
    that saturday
under the shadows of el grids
with six tray under construction
    the men pulling up the green hornets tracks
and the people of saturday getting coloreder
      as we went west
    into the furtile crescent
      ingleside drexel maryland
we heard our messiah and knew him that day
    in bright sun

and he shall come clouded in veild seen by none but a child
    on the records speaker
      above little bruces shop
    dwee doot a leet boy dwee dootalee bop
        dweedootaleebaoohbaa
    bird sang massiahic
      clear at last

[137]

doo yee dee daa
there wre objects of the early forties on the streets
the buick with the dyna flow holes
wopdaaaeeeeyaalaaadeebop
and i looked at the cashmere sweater

with the stomachs hole
and realized that i wouldnt be
a 19 year old fat failure fullback
and we being whom we were
should never have spoke in english
"white pot   dark pot   mus i tell"
"bordeau   burgandy   mums baby"
"pernod anyone"

so the songs led us
"hit that jive jack"
led us
"voot nay on the voutnay"
and we spoke in those years saying
"the ghost acapulco gold"
"donde este la mote"
"bennydexiesaggie"
"morph man   meth man"
"knick and we trip"
"Meth monster"
and we laughed
now we wre so intelligent we spoke saying

"dialotte diaxoxen demarol"
"crystal" we had learned to say
    and we were so religious
        we repeated the alphabet
        and so courageous
        we took on the magic dragon
    then allah came over filthy processed streets
and layed outside the white boys window
        he wasn't long for doom
and pointed the stranger his buildings of gold
    then we were with malady in their infirmarys
they wrote stelezine prolixin anti depressent
        like dead potato plants we were drug
    and they said
        "six hun-zred liquid scorzine or hydro"
        the ricke said
          "choke that basterd out"
    but we spit at them
        in the prisons our mothers loved
    till our eyes gave blood
when they wrote electricity
        and we said
    "No god" at last
danced like snow flake
          even said
    "thank yo boss"
        and took to the alleys
        how could they know we had won it in our mecca

now we have forgotten
the hypo points on reel cable tables in san francisco
        forgotten when we were super hip
        and said
        "lemme snort peter quill"
and now there is a greenback disaster almost here
and we have walked the south side in blue fezes
    like the muslims we are always
            and if you hear us coming
        but you never will
    until we 'make you out of stone'
            this love
        and if you hear us coming
baadaapbaadeebeeeyaadaa daaadaaatdaadeedeeeyaadaa
doobaaaooodaapdoooyadaa deedoopdaadeeedoooyabaaaa
AS IT WAS IN THE BEGINNING
AS IT WAS IN THE BEGINNING AND EVER SHALL BE WORLD
                        WITHOUT END AMEN

        we are the hipmen
        going into sun
        stand up against us
        mister gog youre done
        where are we going
        into the sky

halt our boggie
and a continients shy
we are the hipmen
singing like black doves
why were we sent here
only to love

The Coming Of John

(the evening and the morning were the first day)

it is friday
the eagle has flown
4 years before the real god Allah shows
before we know the happenings
we eat the devils' peck
mondays hotlinks with porkenbeans
hear "newk" on dig and "bags" on moonray
see desolation in the dark between the buildings
our front view is bricks of the adjacent kitchenette

Pat riffs in a babyfied key
slips on the green knit suit
with the silver buckle at the belly
and we slide out into that wintertime
the last lights of day
with an uncanny clarity for chi town
the shafts behind the clouds popping them open
and the rust on the el grids
clashing and blending strangely
against the rays like hip black art

heaven about to show itself
above the ghetto holiday shoppers
the 1954 brand fragments of people on the walks
hadacol on her way north
after officer driseldorf has stomped her on the street
and crushed her finger on a golden ring

the hipster in the tivoli eat shop
deals single joints after the commotion
dusk baring his first meal
with us steaming and talking about the guns
getting so mad and so frantic we sweat
get on to cool
go on home
make love and nod
then it is the new year
and the guns are going off across the alley

10 days or so hes still "on this end"
only Edwardo Harris knowing his name
John Coltrane (as he was called then)
in a big hat
gouster pleated pants and all
before metamorphosis miles plugs cotton in his ears
and philadelphia thunders in babylon
a shake dancer follows the set
and it seems a whole sea of black faces are out on "six trey"
a holy nation peeping and poor
behind the red oblong bulb of a highlife sign

Ohnedaruth the mystic has already blown and hypnotized
us—

making us realize right then
THAT WE ARE LIVING IN THE BIBLE (HOLY KORAN, CABALA)

the kenatechi girl sits there frozen
shes followed her lifelong scent of judea

[143]

from the rich north shore township
all the way into the crown propeller lounge
into a blessed tenors bell
while we go "off into space"
peeping the dream of the old ladies of nipon
dragging the bags of brown smack across the dead
                                                battlefields
chanting "fun amelikaan" "fun amelikaan" "fun joo"

"All right, na iss a party. Ya dig that. Na Miles come and be doin all la rights thangs ya understand. Take the hordevures from the lazy susan with so much finese. An be so correct when when he be talking to them big fine socialite Hos. They be sayin 'Oh Miles', understand.

"Na here come Trane. He wrong from the get go Reach his hand down in the tray. Say 'gimme one of them little samaches'. He done pushed the pushed the mop out the way, took the jonny walker red way from one of the Ivy league dames and drank it down out the bottle. An Miles see he diggin him. He his man, he brought the man in here for that. They working together, understand.

"What the man is tryin ta tell ya wit his horn, is that you all can't get nowhere being what the bray call intell gent. If yall want to get somewhere in america, ya gotta start bustin down dos and shit. Knocking these lames upside the head. Pitchin a fit. Laying these peckerwoods out cross the room is whas go getchu somewhere in america. Now if y'all don't start, letting yall's wigs grown wild and shit and start gettin' all up in greys faces, just like me and like mau maus. Africa an sixty third street ain't no different. Y'all ain't going another futher, understand. Because this shit in this country richere, is all comin down to some head bustin'." Sho anuff.

we stay till the lights
pull the covers off the room
showing the ragged carpet
in the great american tradition
(mayhap a manager)
make in in
fire up two thumbs and sleep
t.i. on a pallet in front of the bad window

and the hotel catches fire
the lobbys all smoking
the few steel workers with their helmets
the several a.d.c. families
the pimps, the hustlers and the chippies
are all milling around out of it
when the "konat girl" turns up in smoke
in just leotards and a mouton coat
now shes took the pressing iron to her slavic hair
(that morning is the second day)

LARRY NEAL

Holy Days

HOLY THE DAYS OF THE OLD PRUNE FACE JUNKIE MEN.
HOLY THE SCAG FILLED ARMS.
HOLY THE HARLEM FACES
LOOKING FOR SPACE IN THE DEAD ROCK VALLEYS OF THE
CITY

HOLY THE FLOWERS
SING HOLY FOR THE RAPED HOLIDAYS
AND BESSIES GUTS SPILLING ON THE MISSISSIPPI
ROAD
SING HOLY FOR ALL OF THE FACES THAT INCHED
TOWARD FREEDOM, FOLLOWED THE NORTH STAR LIKE
HARRIET AND DOUGLASS.
SING HOLY FOR ALL OUR SINGERS AND SINNERS
AND ALL OF THE SHAPES AND STYLES AND FORMS
OF OUR LIBERATION,
HOLY, HOLY, HOLY, FOR THE MIDNIGHT HASSLES
FOR THE GODS OF OUR ANCESTORS BELLOWING
SUNSETS
AND BLUES CHANTING THE TRUTH THAT GAVE US VISION
O GOD MAKE US STRONG AND READY
HOLY, HOLY, HOLY FOR THE DAY WE OPEN OUR EYES, DIG
OURSELVES
AND RAISE IN THE SUN OF OUR OWN PEACE AND PLACE AND
SPACE; YES LORD.

The Way It Went Down

Baby   looking at it that way from here
I knew   from the get-go that it all
had to go down that way   night blows smack
                        eerie rain
                        eases in from the sea
and dig baby   even the magnolias were singing   so   so
                                                    so
I knew even then   even in the cup of your body
I knew   the kitchen smelling banana bread   and do
short ribs baking
knew even then
turning down the light
and my hands between your thighs
and wet stars
knew
easing in wind sea
magnolias singing
rain swings in from the sea   I knew
then   cup of body and night blown smack   dig baby
looking at it this way from here   and don't forget
don't forget the   don't forget the   movie and the late ooze
                                                    of love

Knew that it might go down that way
and the bed flying in space   wet stars knew
baby looking at it from here righteously

it had to go down that way
it had to
it had to
it had to go down that way
and the late ooze of love breathing O
ooze
light
wind sea
cool night mama
but I knew it
way down to go
and the day we ended it
way go down   to go   we had to
end it   forget   don't please

rainy thighs
cup of bodies
space   somebody stopped singing in our world
somebody stopped singing   magnolias
stopped singing near the window in our world
so
naturally it had to go down that way
the rivers swelled putrid
and eerie

the rollers blasted Reggie on the avenue
and Herbie
you know Herbie died of o.d.

it was a particularly awful day
that's why I knew it had
to go down that way

DAVID   NELSON

Essie Mae

". . . And see her image in the river . . ."
                              —Waring Cuney

Mama!
            Fine Foxy Mama
Wearing the thorny crown of christ
                  Carved outta steel
Not looking ahead to
                  golden future
                              Shafts of lite   cuttin cross
                        the river
Never seeing Stars encircling you
            Being yourself Stars
                  Stars
                        Star

                  HEY

            Fine Foxy Mama
Walkin down John R
            Shake dat thang little girl
OOOOOOOOOOOOO—Weeeeee
            LOOKA DER.
                        Where?
            Right 'cross der
            Hip shakin Mama
Mama!
      Mama.

      [154]

Mama . . .
Titties hangin dry
Your proud beauty gon limp
                    in the Springtime. . . .
Stretched out on a cross to die
            Don't die mama   Reach out for the Sun
Dance yesterday's dried up laughter
Against tomorrows dreams   Dream Mama
            Dream Mama   Dream Mama   Awww Mama

                                        DREAM

DREAM MAMA
Struttin tall down John R
            Nigga turn heads   peekin
        Loud black eyeballs—follow hip shakin you

OOOOO—OOOH!
                    Too Much
Hey baby   You sho look good
Say hi yella   You sho look mella
Why don't you jump in my chine
                        Know what I mean?

Awww   Baby don't cut me loose
                        I'll give you some of this love juice
Awww Mama!

            Dream Baby!
            Baby!

    [155]

Baby!
Baby!
Baby!
Baby!
Baby!
Baby/Dream Babies

Black dream boy dancin in your arms
Love pressed between your thighs . . .

Mellow love queen   Pussy tite bitch
Ache and Cry
Ache and Cry
CRY

Then scream

EEEEEEEEEE—OOOOOOOOOOO!
EEEEEEEEEE—OOOOOOOOOOO!

OOOOOOOOooooooo
OOOOOOOOooooooo

Ahhh . . . . . a . . . . . . Awwww   Mama

LOVE DRIPPIN THRU SPACE
THE FIREY COMET SHOT FROM GOD'S CANNON
DREAM STARS MOVIN IN
YOUR BED OF CRIES AND SCREAMS
MOANS IN THE GOLDEN RIVER

EGYPTIAN QUEEN
INDIAN PRINCESS

GODDESS OF TIMELESS STARS

> Big legged
> ho
> walkin
> down
> John R

Dream . . . black dream
Look out at the sun
Tomorrow is here
Purple clouds wrapped
     round your head

Soft chimes
     hum in the breeze

Black Indian Princess

    Bathe in the Timeless glowing river . . .

And the Sun
And the Sun
And the Sun
And the Sun

ARTHUR PFISTER

The Funny Company (or, why ain't him and his girls on t.v.?)

like
i can't say
that they're

—whatchacallits—

　　　or

—whatchamacallums—

but
Batman had
. . . Robin
& Superman
definitely had a thing
with Batman
(i mean, they even got funny-*books* together)

Matt Dillon
had
. . . Chester
the Cisco Kid
had
. . . Pancho
　　　　(*OO-OO-OO-OO-OOOOOOH* Cisco!)
　　　　(oo-OO-oo-OOOOOOOOOOH! Pancho!!!)

&
the Lone Ranger
had
. . . Tonto
Tarzan had
. . . "boy"
& a monkey
(& Jane couldn't move the *monkey* out!)

Roy Rogers
had
Nelliebelle, bullet, & Trigger
and some cat whose name
i don't even *remember!*

Kennedy
had
"bruther baubee"

Oedipus
had
his *momma!*
&
j. edgar hoover
                    got the
                            faggot
                                    b.
                                        i.

Poem & ½ for Blackwomen
(with apologies for mussin' wi' de cussin')

1 letter!   2 letter!   3 letter!   4!

u-can-do-it-for-days-'till-yieau-"thang"-gets-sore!
ucanfuckit
ucanfuckit
ucanfuckit
ucanfuckit

ufuck *wilma* and *gumbi* and val and cess
(the sister with *three* o' them "things" on her chest)

fuckin' june and anne and mary and toni
(u'd even fuck the bones off bony-maroni)
ucanfuckit
ucanfuckit
ucanfuckit
ucanfuckit

fuckin' mattie and hattie and susie and cassie
(if i'd call u a dog, u'd probably fuck *lassie*)
fuckin' flora and cora and cathie and annie
(u'd probably put yieau "thang" in the *flyin' nuns fanny*)
ucanfuckit
ucanfuckit
ucanfuckit
ucanfuckit

fuckin' itha and eva and martha and suttha
and after *that* u'd fuck yieau mutha
—muthafuck*aaaaaaaaaaaa*

        "a-dog-can-fuck
        a-*bull*-can-fuck
        the-cow-who-jumped
        o-ver-the-moon
        can-fuck. . . . ."

if he wasn't so huge, and his booty wd part-right
u'd think it yieau *duty* to fuck *HOSS CARTWRIGHT!!!*
ucanfuckit
ucanfuckit
ucanfuckit
ucanfuckit

fuckin' nancy and maggie and vickie and nikki
(if u was skinny, no-kneed olive oil
u'd fuck popeyes' hickey. . . . .)
u'd fuck *FA-FA-FA-FA-FA-FA-FA-FA-FA*
u'd fuck *SHOO-BEE-DOO-BEE-DOO-BEE-DOO-BA-*
      DAAAAAYYY
u'd fuck *DOO-WACKA-DOO-WACKA-DOO-WACKA-*
      DOO!!!!!!!!

if they were *here,* and weren't over *there*
u'd fuck the *BEE-TOLES*
'till they'd holler-   "yeah
                yeah
                        yeah . . ."

[163]

if *he* had a "thing" between *his* lil' toses
u'd jump in yieu bible and try to fuck *MOSES*
ucanfuckit
ucanfuckit
ucanfuckit
ucanfuckit

and *"GEORRRRRRRRRRRRRGE O' DE-JUNGLE"*
(watch out for his "thi-i-i-i-i-ing!")

ucanfuckit
ucanfuckit
ucanfuckit
ucanfuckit

funckin' mollie and jennie and wanda and tutie
(with the teeny-weeny 'fro and the howdy-doody booty)
fuckin' lula and edith and carol and florence
(if u was in arabia, u'd probably fuck *lawrence*)
if u was a hoss and u wasn't no nigger
u'd get yieau jollies offa' fuckin' *trigger*
if u was just a lil'-lil' teeny bit sicka
u'd go on 'head and fuck *my-friend-flicka!*
ucanfuckit
ucanfuckit
ucanfuckit
ucanfuckit

if u didn't think *grey* bitches was hipper
u'd swim the pacific, tryin' to fuck *flipper!*
ucanfuckit
ucanfuckit
ucanfuckit
ucanfuckit

u'd fuck a *pilot* a *seabee* a *U.S. marine!*
(*then* u'd go on 'head and fuck
the-bitches-in-the-middle-of-*PLAYBOY*-magazine)
ucanfuckit
ucanfuckit
ucanfuckit
ucanfuckit

fuckin' martha and minnie and tinne and *ting*
(grandma' pushin' 80, with *her* dried-up "thing")
fuckin' eulah and beulah and zannie and cass
(the alabama yamma with the rubberized ass)

ucanfuckit
ucanfuckit
ucanfuckit
ucanfuckit

fuckin' bunny and betty and bertha and carol
(u'd *try to* put yieau "thang" in cosbys wiiierd harold)

ucanfuckit
ucanfuckit
ucanfuckit
ucanfuckit

if i'd stand on my head and sing "oh-say-can-u-see"
u'd go on head and try to fuck *me!*

ucanfuckit
ucanfuckit
ucanfuckit(yt-boy suckit)
ucanfuckit(ucan squeezit)
ucanfuckit(ucan teeeezit)
ucanfuckit(jabandstab)
ucanfuckit(pushandshove)
ucanfuckit
ucanfuckit
ucanfuckit
. . . can
    u
    l
    o
    v
    e
    .
    .
    .
    ?

CLARENCE REED

Lemme Tell You What My Black Is All About

my black is about rhythm, sound
soul an hurt an joy
my black is sweat droppin
finger poppin, hallelujah!
booga-a-loo little sister down the street
my black is lumpy beds and
tcb and all the good in life
down to the black bone of god
and moosey and sharon and you and a
sanctified shout at break of day
harambee
big black paul robeson lives
i saw him
i say malcolm lives!
garvey lives!
karenga is
imamu is
preacher king went up on the mountain
and walked to the sun
SHANGO is black thunder
clapped down on trembling honky hearts

my black is about people who
know they saw the birth of time
and touched by god
moved thru death and slavery

centuries long
to stand now, with the night
in one hand, day in the other, saying:
"beast—what will it be"

but later for that
my black is about moosey and sharon
we black
and can't nobody else know what that means . . .

Lord, Girl She Dance, She Dance

under moon under sky
she touch one foot so
she leap and she whirl
she dance to the fire
she dance like so
she dance so slow
hands on she hip
she walk slow in the fire
she laugh, oh lord
she turn in the fire
just so, just so
she ju-ju girl, she know, she know
she smile in the fire
just so, just so
her eyes she brown
her belly round
her thigh be heavy
her smile just so
she ju-ju girl
she know, she know . . .

Cosa Nostra Economics

club baron got niggas goin
juga jug
club baron got turnstile
thru which as goin into heaven
no moneyless sinner can pass

blakey got drums say bama lam
register get happy say clinga ling
blakey say bama lam
niggas go juga jug
turnstile say kluma lum
register say clinga ling
mafia man sing "mr. bojangles"
while he bama lam
juga jug
kluma lum
bama lam
clinga ling to his bank
and he aint even got rhythm
all he got is what he need
a big boom boom

'Trane

there is no night
not where you and clifford dwell
two golden chalices wrought with love
tempered with happiness and tears
burnished by hopeful hands and
thankful lips
dancing in the last sun's light
shine me along the odd and desperate ways

i will not bring
rusted buckets of remorse
contumacious regrets or stiff
polite smiles and careful words—
oh no
i bring memories
of subway sleeping songs
crusted blood and
death 'round the corner ditties
hot womenless prison nights
wine nightmares
and the slow songs of dead mothers

i bring nothing more than
rhapsody and pain
death entwined hope

righteous songs
and the beautiful blackness
of our spirit world

no other but this
not ever where you and clifford dwell. . . .

your song was the comfort of the wind
the honesty of fire, yet
secret deep as the slow-fast river
and it helps us to know
there cannot be night, silence or solitude
where you and clifford dwell . . .

a beautiful and gentle man
as summer wind
a romantic singer of strident cries
raucous whispers of hope and hurt
      and prayer

the wind cannot hold you
nor rivers mock your shifting depth
the day dare not claim you
nor night reveal your tears

CAROLYN RODGERS

Together

Sitting in a candle lit room
warm from tip top top
Incense sweating like burning leaves or fresh peanuts
oven baked.
five of us, we rap, sit, get high
and I put Sly on the box
and we rock, moan, close our eyes
pop our fingers, off on a trip. together . . .
with some secret separate precious remembrance

and Smokey cries out
and we laugh-too funny
and someone light another reefer and another
and we smoke—down—

and Aretha and the Tempts stretch us out
until we are laying all over the floor
in a haphazard fashion.

Our eyes are sometimes open and we look at each other
Occasionally, we speak. We rap, smile
and we are laying so very close . . . we dig . . .

                    But no one hears another
                    No one sees each-other
                    and though we are oh so close
                         we   do   not   touch

Only the vibrations screammmmmm.

We are, all,   inside ourselves.

Alone.

Tired Poem/Slightly Negative/
MORE POSITIVE!

i
am
tired . . .
so tiiiiiiredd
nothing matters
except everything—
anymore.
all my dreams
have been dreamed
redreamed and redreamed
and they are tired too.
yeah, even my dreams
are too tired to move me.
i
am
lonely.
and used to it
lonely don't bother me
no more—
except when it do.
i been lonely by my self
i been lonely with my self
with other people,
i been lonely by myself
with one person so close
couldn't tell which was who
lonely.

and used to it.
and it don't bother me/
except when it do . . .
i
am
old
and young
so old
new ain't new and nothing happening
is reaaaally nothing happening!
but so young
i can see so much, so old
i can't dance the current beat
no mo
young enough to want to
but it don't bother me when i can't.
it don't even excite me when i can!
i'm tired and young and old
none of it phase me . . . . . .
except when it do

i
am
dissssss-a-pointeddd d
yeah.
i ain't changed much.
was Black and didn't know it
is Black and now i know it
was Black when i wasn't is Black,
hell, i ain't changed much.

and Black folks ain't changed
ENOUGH—
ain't nothing realllllly happening . . .

Black folks
ain't goin no-where
soon.
ain't about re-vo-lu-shun
no kinda way
folks is hangin on, hangin in, hangin out, hangin around
they jest tired
and young old old young
and lonely
and confused
and don't know where to go
or how to git there
and everything matters
to everybody
except when it don't.

and sometimes i feel that
that ain't often enough for folks
to work
and be happy and Black together

and if something!
great day in the outhouse, usa
don't happen soon soon soooon
one late or early
lord, god, allah,

morning or night or hour or second or minute!
            i'm gon lay down, lay me down on the earth.
                 and quake and
crake up/in a flood of tears, from east to west—
and *everybody* gon have to get busy
and stand together and *fight*
            just to keep from drowning . . . dying

                     . . .
            in ME.
a CRAKING FLOWING FLOODING FREEDOM
        VIBRATION.
          yes indeed.
           let the congregation say, *a-men* . . .

For O.–Two Hung-up

For Us

i think
   we probably
     love each other
        since we
       can't stay apart.
          yet
everytime
       you come around
         i feel the pain
       the spirit
          moving
       in my flesh

     our eyes shine a gloss too much
        all the jokes we share
       could not be as funny as
       how long we laugh
   we laugh
        so hard
        we cry
and between the jokes and laughs and tears
we parry with word foils that leave tiny holes, aches, wounds

and i always feel like
i could take you or leave you
especially when you ain't here.
but you keep coming back
keep coming back
and i keep asking why
though everytime i open the door and
see your face
i know the why.
and then we start,
the jokes
the laughing
the fencing & the aching & the tears
and when you leave i always say
Please, don't come back
and you always say just as if i never opened my
mouth
"see you next time"
and i think if you didn't say that each time i would
die . . .
but each time when i close the door
after you are gone i cry
and sit and wonder and know and cry
why?

All the Clocks

All the clocks
   are
      off
or have stopped in
      the Black ghetto
Some say it's 6 when it's 3
      4 when its 2
10 when it's 8 . . .

It occurs to me.
      The people in the (neighbor) hoods
            don't
            know
            what
               TIME
                  it is . . .

SONIA SANCHEZ

Queens of the Universe

Sisters.
            i saw it to
                        day.   with
My own eyes.
                        i mean like i
got on this bus
                        this cracker wuz
driving saw him look/
                        sniff a certain
smell and
            turn his head in disgust.
sisters.
            that queen of sheba
                        perfume wuz
dooooooooing it.
                        strong/
                                    blk/
                                    smell that it
be. i mean
            it ain't delicate/stuff
sisters.
            when u put it on
                        u be knowing it on.
so naturally.
            i sits down rt behind him
                        and let the

smell of the nile/
                watusi/
                        shango/
big/ass/blk/women
                      irritate his
white/guts.
           sisteeeerrrs, when i got
up to leave
           he be so grateful
                     he didn't
even mind that
            i forgot
                to drop 35¢
in the money/eating/machine.
                       yeah.
sistuhs. let us where our blk/smells
strong
      ly
        to offend
    all white noses
sniffing
        after
            the most
beautiful/perfume of
the world.   US.
                Blk/women
the only queens of this universe

To Morani/Mungu

As-Salaam-Alaikum my black princes
the morning awaits u.
     the world
awaits yo/young/blackness
sun/children
    of our tomorrow.
Here is my hand
     black/warriors of
our dreams.
    it is soft as the
blue/nite that covered yo/
blackness
    till day began its
morning talk.
    it is hard as
the strength u gather from
yo/father's words pouren
from his mouth like thunder
over a dry land.
    but i am
here to love u my princes.
     to gather
up yo/insides
    and make them
smile dreams.
    for u my loves

will be the do/ers.
                   and yo/deeds
will run red with ancient songs
that play a continuous chant of
it's a new day.
                it's a new new new day
              It's a NEW DAY!
As-Salaam-Alaikum
    young princes.
                the world
awaits yo/young/blackness

To Anita

high/yellow/black/girl
walken like the sun u be.
move on even higher.
                              those who
laugh at yo/color
                    have not moved
to the blackness we be about
cuz as Curtis Mayfield be sayen
we people be darker than blue
                              and quite a few
of us be yellow
                    all soul/shades of
blackness.
              yeah. high/yellow/black/girl
     walk yo/black/song
          cuz some of us
                    be hearen yo/sweet/music.

don't wanna be

don't wanna be
no pimp
        cuz pimps hate me and you
        they mommas, women, sistuhs too
        u name it, any hate will do

don't wanna be no pimp no mo
don't wanna be no pimp no mo

don't wanna be
no numbers runner
        cuz runner promise an uptown hit
        while downtown wite/boys just siti & sit
        while counting millions of four bits

don't wanna be no numbers runner no mo
don't wanna be no numbers runner no mo

don't wanna be
no junkie
        cuz junkies kill theyselves, you and me
        sticking needles in they arms, legs, knee
        while robbing our black community

don't wanna be no junkie no mo
don't wanna be no junkie no mo

Just wanna be
                    a/Reverend/Cleage/man
                    a/Minister/Farrakhan/man
                    a/sun/people/Imamu/man
                an/Elijah/Muhammad/Messenger/man

wanna be
                    a/blk/man
                    a/loving/my blk/woman/man
                    a/standing/still/Father/man
                a/Constant/T C Bing/black man

it gots to beeeEEE. yeah. yeah. yeah.
it gots to beeeEEE. yeah. yeah. yeah.

WELTON SMITH

A Sequence from *The Roach Riders,* a Play

ANCESTORS CHANT : What-chu gon' do wid tis boy
he don' know night
he don' know day
What-chu gon' do wid tis boy
he know street light
he know street light
What-chu been teachin' dis boy
Who been teachin' dis boy
Who you come from, who you come
from
What-chu gon' do wid tis boy

ENSEMBLE BOP CHORUS : PO-LEEZ PO-LEEZ don't put no
one man 'hind-tha blame
This time's here, that time's blowed
away
eat what-chu can ta'night, eat
what-chu can ta-day.
PO-LEEZ don't put no one man
'hind-tha blame.
FIRE don't burn that lady's house
FIRE TRUCK do his
best.
SUPER light-up that lady's house
JUNKY do-tha rest.
PO-LEEZ don't tell me one man be
that bad.

PO-LEEZ PO-LEEZ PO-LEEZ
PO-LEEZ PO-LEEZ

DUET: Don't give no mess
Don't take none neither
Yo' mama jet black
And got White Fever.

SOLO: Who grows the subway flowers
Who puts the cats in heat
Who grows the German Shepherd
Who do-dos on my street

ENSEMBLE BOP CHORUS: PO-LEEZ PO-LEEZ don't put no
man 'hind-tha blame.
PO-LEEZ PO-LEEZ don't put no
man 'hind-tha blame.
PO-LEEZ PO-LEEZ PO-LEEZ
PO-LEEZ

DUET: Teen-agers 'sposed to be so smart
Maybe not and Maybe—
How come sister don't use no
protection
How come she have a baby
That's smart? It ain't to me
To me it's silly
What I look like eight-years old
Bein' somebody's Uncle Billy.

ENSEMBLE BOP CHORUS: PO-LEEZ don't grab me off the
                                        street
                        PO-LEEZ don't deny me time to eat
                        PO-LEEZ don't choke my neck with
                                        charm
                        PO-LEEZ don't put that needle in
                                        my arm.
                        PO-LEEZ don't let no one man be
                                        that bad.

                SOLO: How come little Puerto Rican girls
                        Like to act so mannish
                        Come grabbin' at my ding-a-ling
                        And laffin' all that Spanish.

                SOLO: Roaches is people too
                        'cept they little and don't take up
                                        much room
                        When roaches see-tha people
                                comin' tryin to squash
                                        them,
                        They go ZOOM.

ENSEMBLE BOP CHORUS: SISTER   SISTER   SISTER
                                SISTER   SISTER
                        They burnin' up her house. SISTER,
                                        put the baby
                        On the Roaches. That Puerto
                                Rican Lady's house's

On Fire. PO-LEEZ PO-LEEZ can't
                nobody stop the roaches.
PO-LEEZ they got-tha Junky out
                         burnin'
down houses. SISTER WAKE UP
Mama say climb on the roaches
Mama say put-tha baby on the
                    roaches.
The streets' all on fire
The Junky burnin' everybody up
PO-LEEZ don't put no one man
                'hind-tha blame
PO-LEEZ don't put no one man
                'hind-tha blame
PO-LEEZ PO-LEEZ PO-LEEZ
           PO-LEEZ PO-LEEZ
PO-LEEZ don't let no one man be
                that bad.

RICHARD W. THOMAS

To the Survivors of Hiroshima and Nagasaki

Bombs they dropped on
you
were wrapped in an American
Dream
in the name of those
They lied to
built by hands
who kicked the Indians
off their earth. Stole a
million black bodies
to brick up the
banks

        and stomp the
folk who swam the
border
to pick the grapes
for the wining and dining
of their

        dream-maker bomber
pilots.

We often wondered
why they dropped the thing
on you

        and not their Nazi
cousins operating the ovens.
But now we know.

They're all part of a family, all
from the same spot of history
like a pale plague.
                    But we didn't always
wonder.   We used to cheer
for John Wayne running up
Hills blowing the "Bad Japs" out of
foxholes; yea! John was our main
man; G.I. Joe, the White hero
saving the world for
a white penis and Chase
Manhattan Bank, the Faggot!
                    Kill the Japs! Kill
the Japs! We used to holler,
in a white theater selling stale
candy to the nigger kids, all
playing white G.I. Joes
killing the bad Japs; yea!
That was our thing then baby,
But we know better now. We know
                    you were bombed twice
because you were niggers, like us,
like everybody on the globe
who don't look like John Wayne. Yea!
                    They had to bomb you
twice because you beat their
butts, you sucker-punched them
at Pearl Harbor
Like they've been sucker-punching
our folk for years, yea! baby.

They bombed you because
your were niggers like the Red niggers,
Black niggers and Brown niggers, they've
been messing over for so long.

       Can you dig it?
think about it
next time they send one of
their little white boys
to rap to you about
other super-jive bags
they're coming from.
          Think about it
and sucker-punch them again
for all the niggers
they're still sucker-punching
around the world!

The Glass Stomach

—to those who know,
to struggle is to be human
and Divine

> Shouts we shouted
> are dead
> shouts now
>   nothing
> has changed.
>
> Same twisted alleys:
> intestines seen through
> a glass stomach.
>
> Young trees
> smiling green, high
> and light
> teasing with a cold
> death
> its short memory blocks
> out
>
> Wonder where they all
> will be next year?
> Married?
> Crippled?
> Dead from sudden exposure
> to the light
>   Walking dead,

Spreading deaths which
seem hip?
Out of some islands
beyond postage routes or jumbo
jets, educational T.V.
People crawl up to their surfaces
create new myths, crucifixes,

Force subscriptions on the already hip.
Kill, maim them
if they don't subscribe.
      Even though they know:
surfaces crumble when shouts can't deliver
    a new day, but only hunger
    for that day.
      Suppose that day is a lie,
plastic rabbits
on a grey round race track, moving
everytime we get closer,
      Suppose . . . And die!
And die, either inside
or out, with a thud, explosion or
a signalless whimper
like a dead puppy popped open,
red, on a four lane highway.
If we could only touch the side
of the sun.
Evenings when it turns red
stands still for us.
      If only

we could love without burying ourselves
in hot jail-like bodies
that we hate after
all animal is gone, while
like two corpses
we drag ourselves to opposite
holes
to vomit up
the garbage we called love.

On a billboard
he holds a gun. On a page
20 miles up
she undresses, props her legs up
and receives half a need, needing
a universe.
      On a bright day, he jumps,
places his 38 to his head,
prays, kisses his child, visits his
mother's grave.
remembers his baby brother
in a plastic bag fresh from Vietnam.
In turn
the bottom of everything thought real
and hip
collapses,
      Looking down. . . .
air, blue eternal air
for miles
down

[205]

not a pinpoint of earth.
Air,
blue,
      clear, red sun burning down
your throat.
Christ and Buddha,
an Americard,
      factories
as cemeteries. Little girls
twisting, boys chasing. Old folk
waiting for the last blackout. . . .
But a tiny army, fully equipped marches on
Beneath the miles of blue air,
      twisting their way through jungles, cities
and holding their rifles high
singing. . . .

JAMES W. THOMPSON

You Are Alms

FOR: *Cecil Taylor, Black composer/pianist & Musicologist*

You are alms—love
—all lilting legs
            lending light
        in shadowed streets;
        strolling benificent
beneath star's steel, morning's mauve,
            noon's amalgamate frenzy;
rain wind and the rage of raucous Rotarians
realing to unwind from the stupor of acquisition
            in an alcohol-acquired feel
                of ready red-bloodedness
and rage; rage for your alms, your acquisition
                being the essential (yourself)
                not bi-leveled rooms
                    attached
                entombed.

You are alms—love
—the lyricism of the living,
        unfettered even in your needs
            strolling benificent
            lending light
to pallid thugs hunched on corners
            hopping in frantic step:
the brown posture—clutching, anguished,
        at their acquisition of manhood
            (not being men but postures to penises attendant);

in envy without knowledge of need which makes being
   vital, and acquistion—an attendant factor
               of living—
        not itself a life;
without knowledge of why the language of African
        or Red Indian—wedded in a mellow mouth
          raised an idiom
          and an esthetic felt,
               formulated through the ritual
of maintaining life in the outrageous streets of the settlers.

You are alms—love
—raised in an idiom and an esthetic
       felt and formulated
     before the brain could record the feeling
         in the introspective isolation of intellect
   to art, attending:
            yours is the art and record of itself
and though time visits the vital with remonstrances
   art is the living—not the dead.

And There Are Those

To an actual someone,
some long time ago. . . . .

There are many
who deny themselves;
you are one.
You are not
a Black woman;
On your lips
one tastes
a gaul
proscribed
in melodies—Mozart,
in brittle Barber
made efficacious
by a Leontyne
whose womanhood
transforms antiques
into active backgrounds
for her relief.
Settings,
my dear,
so that one
might hear
her mastery of pasts,
presently rendered.

Speaking of cultures,
colors coalesced
in co-option

by Caucasians—corrupted:
You have slendered
yourself for onslaught
not against systems
but self.
We are *all* brothers,
but Brother Charles
has his hand in my pocket;
his gift has been a rope
as locket for my throat—
shackles to mar
my ankles
a gag to stiffle
my shouts—
these
are his SEALE
of silence.

Brother Charles,
has a mean mouth
poised to taste
my genitals.
He's sane,
sanctimonious,
safe in suburbia
with lily of valley
who has not
been laid.
Brother Charles
sleeps with the maid

and pumps his predatory queen
to produce more
proper people!
You, he makes
a prostitute without
papers—
you receive
no pay!

You are not
a Black woman.
You slender
for an onslaught
against self,
balancing in Bach—
not Bobby Blue Bland,
B. B.   Billie, Betty Carter
Coltrane or Coleman—Hawkins
or Ornette;
You're tre avant garde,
glace supreme.
In basic black
pearls
moonlight your throat,
as you bow
to gods not *your* own.
Appreciation of other
cultures *is* commendable.
Burying ones blackness
in snow

puts a freeze
on the soul:
denies the ancestors continuance
in celebration of the culture.
Keeping customs
is love of self—
life's principle.
To revere one's past
is to rule one's present.

You are not
being present.
People
who danced pavannes
are dead.
Their ancestors
protracted their histories,
and you believed them
forgetting BESSIE—
ignoring Aretha,
Ruth Brown
DIANA—
Dorothy Maynor
is a misnomer
to you.
You are not
a continuance
of your culture.
You're a conflicted
acculturation

without awareness—
dealing in abstracts,
all amorphous clouds
kaleidoscopes of
phantom images.

And Black youths
beat tatoos
in Ghettos
with tin cans
on stone.
Black men
fall in scarred streets
of crusted cities;
lead is their release.
Brothers Black
and Brother white
proffer pities
in reports on VIOLENCE.
Birds no longer
knit morning with their wings,
but hover hanging crepe,
as you hang your head
in Bach's
Missa Solemnis—
a Missa Luba
is much too strange.

You are not
a Black woman.

Anger in you
is polite discourse
You are not
a Black woman.
You are become
a mime
of facetious manners,
a shade
reflecting nothing.
You deny your light
yet you do not gain
the other.
Shots are needed
to change your color.
Leopards change
their spots
these days
Our new technology
has ways
to keep
the DEAD alive.
Frankenstein
we thought
was a fictive freak.

And our fathers
spoke of spirits
kept alive
by tap roots
from an ancient tree—

deep in foliage
where earth's blackness
sucked blood
of bodies
left to carrion birds
and carniverous beasts.
You balance in Bach,
a stiff mannikin
captured in VOGUE
—pentacled odalisque—
praising *another's* past.
Models are easily
handled
and after use,
tossed into piles
of past pretences,
projections—pallid.

You are not
a Black woman.
You slendered
for onslaughts
against your past.
a discontinuance of action
analysed into non-existence,
or thrown in a tantrum
to gain attention.
Insufficient self
culls support
in struggles to save

the suicide—the *mean*—
without committment.
LOVE is ACT—
not mouthed decree;
You don't know
yet, about the Bee!
who dips into the systole.
He does not beat
upon the leaf
or pound the petal,
he digs
HONEY.
Strength's never tested
in displays of weakness,
performed as psycho-drama;
This aint no stage.
You aint no actress.
Were I to cut your throat
you'd die—unremembered
except in *this* song.
There are those who
deny themselves—
YOU ARE ONE.

ASKIA MUHAMMAD TOURÉ

Notes from a Guerilla Diary

(for Marvin X & Che Guevara)

"Yes, I'm for peace, and there will be peace—
after the fight!"

                           —*Marvin X*, Proverbs

I wanted to be an artist in my youth.
A great artist, moving in the monumental rhythms
of the Mexicans—Orozco, Rivera, Siqueiros.
I would fill the walls of Africa with brilliant images:
Ebony splendor from the birth of Adam to the pyramids
of knowledge rising from the Soul of Timbuktu.
I would rather, now, be an artist safe in a small loft-
womb, with a warm, brown sun glowing down on me from
her canopy of love: my brown sugar-woman moving
                undulating hips
across the Niger valleys of our dreams.
But there's the Beast with his cancer-spreading nightmare
riding the twisted backs of humankind.
The dying millions: hollow eyes of Fear, bloated bellies,
Hunger-pangs from Mississippi, India, Brazil . . . or
                anywhere that
gentle Dark folks long to lead simple dignified lives.
A peasant wail. A jungle scream. A ghetto junkie-nod.
And then, the Gun in your voice! your walk! your eyes!
glaring in guerilla-glow, the burning cities of your mind
light a torch for the blind unbelievers to grope away
from Europe—longing to chase the shadows from the sun.

I wanted to be a magician in my youth. To call ancient forces
up from the netherword of Myth; to use these forces for
my brothers with mighty imaginations, riding magic carpets
to the stars.
To wizard the valleys and mighty rushing rivers of the Soul;
to fling the flame of Never up the mountains of Beginning;
turn the hills of Wonder into forests for simple lovers.
I wanted to be an artist, before revolution turned me
            towards
Islam and Malcolm's eyes glowing with compassion over
            dope-
infested ghettoes of our fears.
Yes, dreams are beautiful . . . nutmeg sugar . . . but
            Reality's blonde
wig smothers the Afros of our souls;
the mini-skirted Present shoots skag into the morning dews
rising from the flowers of our eyes;
the poison-aired Present prostitutes our vision, pimps away
the honey of our youth.
And so, the Gun glinting coldy in the shadows of our eyes—
Che Guevara and the Mau-Mau stalking forests where
            brown,
naked lovers used to dance.
Guerilla Song wild and wailing in the screams of Pharaoh
            Sanders,
Eastern Crescents glowing like machetes above the
            money-eating
faggots, farting in the face of the world.
I wanted to be an artist, but Allah took my heart and tuned it

for the Jihad of this Age.
Alone, at dawn, I took to the East for the trumpets of Islam,
which will free my son, Tariq, and millions who will move
towards the palm tree of Beauty; once the earth becomes a
      Paradise
where are can flourish with the simple peasant song.
Meanwhile, back to cutting throats and cleaning guns; even
      that
can be a form of art!

Dago Red

(*A Harlem Snow* Song*)

Summer in Harlem in bright tropical colors:
Blackfaces alive in hot pinks/flaming reds/golden orange
crowning strong Blackbodies in rhythm in motion like a
constant boogaloo, a James Brown masterpiece, a drumsong
in colorful Harlem—ebbing and flowing rising and falling
in summertime, hot sweaty summertime in our captive
       pain-years.
But winter is present and snow is falling over Harlem
       rooftops,
hallways, down basements tenements swirling blizzards:
cold chill winter-death being brought to you raw—the New
       Hawk-
in-summer—by the same people who brought you
       Prostitution
Gambling Numbers Bootleg Likker in livid color:
       The Wop Machine
       Wop Machine
       Wop Machine
turning out nodding niggas turning out nodding zombies,
imitating arctic slowdeath. It's Snowing! It's Snowing!
all over Harlem, Philly, D.C., Detroit, Chicago, L.A.
'Frisco, Atlanta, Birmingham and all points north and south
of misery. Snow-blindness   Snow-madness   Snow-death!
in the summertime for you Blackman/woman/child; in yo
       schools,
churches, lodge halls, the Wop Machine operates turning
       brothers

into robot-killers, queens into nodding hoes. Brought to you
in roach-infested color by the same people who brought you
Mussolini/Rizzo/Imperiale/Addonizio/Al Capone:
> *The Wop Machine*
> *Wop Machine*
> *Wop Machine*
in pasty spaghettini white, in Sicilian grey,
in neon mini-skirted rainbows, in blonde-wig platinum,
hepatitis yellow, syphilis green, cardshark/loanshark blue,
in bloody-murder dago red;
The Wop Machine, Wop Machine, Wop Machine
killing yo daddies/mamas/sistas/brothers/CHILDREN,
killing us ALL, Blackpeople—our Nation our Future
> freeeeezing
in a slow nod, blonde wig plastered on a devastated head
> hiiiiigh
above a greasy mini-skirt exposing dirt-encrusted thighs,
running sores, swollen ankles swollen hands, needle-scarred.
The Blackqueen the Greatqueen hooking johns in the dark
> streets
for skag/pimp money; the Blackqueen pissing in her
> drawers
in the dark jungle-streets; in the cold grey dungeons of our
Western captivity when Magic died in our eyes, and we were
> blind
to the cosmic love of our ancestral blueness, resurrected now
and then by a sleepy saxophone, or a hoarse lovely voice
wailing blood-infested shouts of unrequited love—Smokey
> Robinson,
David Ruffin, Jerry Butler, the Ice-man in sweaty summer
> dreams;

but that too another drug competing with skag, likker and
      the
white-christ, if it doesn't raise us or show us our strength—
or the Way out of this living hell!

Snowy Summer   Snowy Summer blown in by the warm
      winds of Italy,
strong sea breezes filled with fresh poppy odors from the
      Turkish
Orient. The New Hawk   the New Hawk   the New
      Hawkers/Hustlers/
Joy-poppers: spaghetti-eating devils goose-stepping once
      again—
Auschwitz, Dachau, Hiroshima, Nagasaki, Sharpville—
      Blackminds
fed into the oven of burning snow; in the hell of yo soul,
an Abdul Rahman sketch of misery in the blizzards of our
      Black-
woof-ticket-selling pain-years, in our shame-years, when our
prophets were murdered in Audubons and Memphis motels
      before
our eyes by contract men in league with the Pentagon, the
      Pope
and the bloody-guinea dago red!

What we gonna do, Blackfolks, what we gonna do?
Muslims, Revolutionaries, Nationalists, Panthers,
what we gonna do?
You, Brother in spun-gold flaming-purple dashiki, slaying
the Beast on t.v. with your fiery tongue, answer the question:
What you gonna do, jive hustler, what you gonna do?

You, Blackqueen in Ashanti super-lappa, turn yo satin-magic
silken gele'd head around and answer the question:
what you gonna do?
O Rev'rend! O Rev'rend! Kingfish T. Pokechops, Bishop
        Adam
Clayton Hogmaws, pull the lady's skirt down and answer the
question: what we gonna do about the Wop Machine, what
        we gonna do?
Miss Booshie! Miss Booshie! Miss Amsterdam News Society
        Column,
put yo mink down and answer my question, girl, what we
        gonna do?
Tricksters and slicksters, mini-skirted cuties, Muslims and
        Soul
station deejays, mothers and brothers and street-corner
        leaders,
how we gonna stop the Snow-storm, what we gonna do?

And while we argue among ourselves—Blacker-than-thou,
bigger/badder-than-thou, richer/slicker/hipper/
        finer-than-thou
The Wop Machine
manufactures frozen zombies by the thousands
The Wop Machine
murders our babies in the dark jungle-streets
The Wop Machine
makes our daily lives a living hell
The Wop Machine
stomps our liberated future in the nuts.

Praised Be His Imminence, the Pope, in snowy-summer-
Mafioso-Red, Ah-Men.
Praised Be His Imminence, the Pope, in snowy-summer-
Mafioso-Red, Ah-Men.
Praised Be His Imminence, the Pope, in snowy-summer-
Mafioso-Red, Ah-Men."

May ten thousand Himalayan mountains, created by our
ghetto junkie-snows, crush him and his top Mafioso
as they screw the faggot-christ† by the hills of
Sicily, in the opiate winds of poppy summer!

NOTES: * "Snow," a word in Blacklanguage meaning heroin.

† "the white-christ," the "faggot-christ": the blonde, nor-
dic idol worshipped by the white, Roman church; not
the great, Black prophet, Isa ibn Maryam (Jesus, son
of Mary).

QUINCY TROUPE

Ode to John Coltrane

With soaring fingers of flame
you descended from Black Olympus
too blow about truth and pain; yeah,

just too tell a story about Black existence.
Than the flames left your fingers and soul,
came winter you laid down
in cold snow
and was cool.

But during bebop filled avante-garde summers
you weaved slashing thunderclaps of sound
weaved spells of hynotic beauty,
blew searing extensions of sublimation.

Trane Trane runaway train smashing all known dimensions
Trane Trane runaway train smashing all known dimensions

Hurtling thru spacelanes of jazz
a Black Phoenix of Third World redeemption.

eye say Trane Trane runaway train smashing all known
*   dimensions*
Trane Trane runaway train smashing all known dimensions

With immortal pure sounds of brotherhood
turning and churning inside you,

boiling and steaming and exploding,
until reaching a stratified piety
whose deity was universal truth

eye say Trane Trane runaway train smashing all known
dimensions
Trane Trane runaway train smashing all known dimensions

In sheets of sounds of injustice
you poured forth the bitter truth, the agony,
the burning pain, but making even that
seem beautiful too

J.C.   J.C.   John Coltrane,   J.C.   J.C.   John Coltrane

You blew your fingers to smoking cinders
preparing for the "Ascension,"
blew beautiful sad death songs
on "Kind of Blue" mornings,
blew love on "A Love Supreme,"
now the ages awaits you,
beyond the infinite darkness
where the 'Bird' of bebop slumbers.

But rage rage rage Coltrane!
Rage against the taking of a vision!
Rage rage rage Coltrane!
Rage against the taking of Life!
For after Life eye know of no other vision.

And there is no guarantee
that one will follow bringing sight
too the place beyond my perception.

But eye concede too time/scarred myth of grand
                possibility,
eye concede to this, but to no more;
cause my life been filled with grand possibilities
but most have shut their doors.
But this be no mere cry of self/pity,
naw, eye dont look at life that way.

Eye am the pessimistic realist
who sees death as final and ugly;
waxed faces, unreal smells in mortuaries;
and flowers that rot upon mounded clay.

If Ojenke or Curtis Lyle were too die
eye would cry. Eye would remember times
that we ate and drank and laughed and chased
beauti/ful Black Women thru streets of Watts together.

Eye would remember new poetry
read in back rooms;
eloquent statements on the pigs inevitable doom:
bringing restoration of the waste of the people,
and that waste resurrected from the dance
upon smoking cinders of love.

Eye see death—as only eye can—
as a hushed kind of deep vast silence,
where roosters never crow
too herald the leaving of deadness,
where the clanking of chains is soundless
when dragged across this bottomless floor;
death is the infinite vigil beyond the door of Life:
death is the lengthening ocean of night
where there shines no light.

Yeah!—eye admit it!—death to me seems forbidding!
Descending into unexplored pits all alone;
pits of inescapable gloom where the air is heavy and dank,
where all flesh has fallen away leaving bones,
and soon the bones are no more,
only the crumbling grave/stone remains
too tell about who you were.

Death is weekends where great hornmen remain silent;
the 'Bird' Lester Young Eric Dolphy Clifford Brown
except on ancient scratched up records
on phonographs of old/timers
who lounge speaking of the good/old days
in delapi/dated or polished rooms.
Those who followed you thru spring
thru summer thru autumn into winter,
those who watched you scatter the phalanx of jazz
and send them reeling and searching for cover,

[233]

those who remember your cry from "Round Midnight"
beauti/ful, esoteric, searing, when it flamed over
the entire sky, prelude too earth shaking thunder and fire
of "Equinox," these friends
who acknowledged your greatness quite early
will weep the hardest and the earliest.

Those who were familiar with your agony.
Those who were familiar with your pain.
Those who felt the hotness of manhood
surge like flames thru their veins, yeah!
these are the ones fear will not claim: they will cry;

"Kulu Se Mama" "Kulu Se Mama" "Ole" "Ole" Coltrane!
"Kulu Se Mama" "Kulu Se Mama" "Ole" "Ole" Coltrane!

Those who felt the prick of hyperdermic death needles
hung off loaded in some shabby dark room,
who drinking wine and dying chased america's illusions
thru cold rank streets steeped in delusion
garbed in the evil mantle of white doom,

who sucked and fucked and jived and shucked
in strait-jacked tombs of insanity,
who came too the game in hopeless pain
and thought his mangled body too be the cobras fangs;
who died just too be doing something different.

Who were witch doctors of intrigue.
Who were voodoo/men of death.
Who were ghosts called hunger.
Who were men called sweat;
not men of 'SEN-SEN' smelling death,
but men of halitosis smelling death!

Who shot 'smack' too ease the pain
of rapes by savages of innocent Black Mothers,
who shot 'smack' too ease the torture
of lynchings by white savages
of noble Black Fathers,
who shot morphine too ease the agony
 of "Blondes have more fun" type Black spinsters.
These ebony maidens who are prostitutes of the soul
who hoped and groped thru the 'Jackie' mystique
went plunging and decadent into the 'Twiggy' mystique;
lost Black beauti/ful Women: chasing images of
        impossibility

while dancin and swingin too the down blues beat
of the philosopher of the Black masses, yeah!
James Brown James Brown Black Brown James Brown!
splendid rhythm of hips that sway
sing you not a song for the Trane?
sing you not a tune of lamentation
for this sacred bard, this jujuman—like you
whose song was about pain and love
and whose heart was very gentle with love?

And you Johnny Mathis, nightingale with the clearest of
        chime,
will you not croon the Trane a line
of love and enduring admiration?

And what of you conceited weavers of rhyme?
You Poets, spilling unfinished drinks
upon the carpets of these times
sitting mesmerized by cheap wine
writing: "Its time its time too write those lines
but I'm too drunk too do it now,
I'll wait until tomorrow too do it,
but its time, its time."

And tomorrow coming and going
leaving unquenchable footprints of yesterday,
and you the fearless warrior-poet
lying stone cold dead in your lead head
gripping an unfinished poem too Trane in your head.

Death has no sympathy for the unfinished.
And of genius and greatness? it feels
not one way or the other.
It simply comes like the exalted thing that it is:
alone, and unescorted into any room—this room perhaps!
bringing news of dimensionless wandering.

Yeah Trane! I'm gonna weep for you!
As will Miles blowing sad songs of style!
As will Poets writing wondrously sad elegies cry!

Yeah! I'm gonna weep for lost and pain Coltrane!
But during moment of future clarity
eye will see you as Black John the jujuman,
Black Phoenix who soared sky high! and even beyond!
breathing love fire light upon a dark vast night
speaking about years of monumental human agony!

Trane Trane John the Baptist, Ohnedaruth,
immortal burning flame of Black jazz,
jujuman running wild over galloping Black Music,
eye give too you this poem of remembrance,
the most sacred gift this poor Black man has.

Trane Trane John Coltrane, you came and while here
breathed light love upon cold red sky
dripping with blood death and fire
so that Black music love
would not falter and die,

eye say rest rest rest Coltrane
Trane Trane John Coltrane
and sleep the deep sleep
of all the ages . . . .

Conversation Overheard

the way they saw it

for Earl Driver, my brother

most people in the world stumble
or drive around 24 hours everyday on a treadmill;
they never move forward one inch;
                              their lives attempt
to scale the absurdities on television;
"no money down all we want is your life!"
says the commercial on the idiot tube
but my love asks me, why are these people walking
around believing that the television is the bible?
and how many of them that voted for
tricky dick nixon ever seen/touched
his living/dead flesh, how many of them
know that agnew has toejam between his toes
after he lies all day on t.v.?
selling suntan lotion with foul breath
thats supposed to make you
a tennis champion, or a golf pro,
or an ohjaysimpson selling chevrolet cars
and running backwards a hundred years
for a touch-back; orangejuicesimpson,
eye thought you said—in college—you wanted
to be a social worker and help underpriviledged
children like yourself
                         is that you on t.v. tryin'
to outrun a corvette on the salt-lake flats!?

[238]

in full football gear with a football
tucked under your brain/your fingers
tryin' to hold on to those "pretty little
green ones," is that you overjoyedsimpson!?
oh well, maybe you will become a movie star
and play sad cow/boys like big jim; a lover?
naw, they'ill never let you play a lover, cause
they're grooming broadway joe namath for that,
anyway, what are these people looking for
that stumble in place on the treadmill?
that kill themselves with five cadillacs—
while millions of people are starving—
in their ten car garages
with only two people—themselves—
in their family, who wear 25 diamond rings
on five stubby fingers
and have 1000 silk suits in their closets
along with 2000 pairs of alligator shoes
that come alive at night and eat up the soggy
brains of their owners, who have spacious
bookshelves with no books on those shelves
and flash hopalong cassidy smiles
out the side of they mouths sayin;
"everything is everything, and
gimme-limme what cha got ta spare"
what is that growing in the test tube in washington
how much makeup does elizabeth taylor wear
how many corsets, how many facelifts has
zsa zsa gabor had, who made up this standard

for beauty anyway? how many movies will linda
kasabian make, how many books will she write?
how come they chained those beautiful black
panther ladies in los angeles and let mansons
tribe of women walk into the courtroom unchained
how many newspapers did the l.a. times sell
for their shit/winning coverage
of angela davis
who is that faggot with a snake for a face
who is that judge with his head blown off
why is his head blown off
who is that drunk with that time bomb
ticking in his pocket
why is that beautiful brother lying dead
in that shot up/bloody chicago deathroom
why hasn't the police shot up
the klu klux klan, the minutemen
the white citizens committee, the birch society
what was the algiers motel and sharpsville all about
who are the 600 families that rule the world
and play chess games of war with whole countries
why is the hour so late and filled with blood
murders, suicides, mad-dogs and com freaks,
why are these people dancing and singing on this treadmill!!??
oh well, eye guess these stupid motherfuckers
will be dancing and singing on this treadmill
for some millions of years to come,

what can a truth seeking poet like me do about it
but go down to the corner
suck in the freshness of some breeze then
go home and make love to my woman

Biographies of the Poets

JOHARI AMINI: Blk/woman/writer/teacher/student . . . born in philadelphia raised in chicago . . . started on my way to blkness in spring 1967 and still travelin to get there . . . treasurer of OBAC (Organization of Black American Culture) and psychology instructor at Kennedy-King College Mini-Campus in chicago . . . working on a new book, *Re-Definition: Concept as Being* (essays). Books of poetry include: *Images in Black, Black Essence,* and *Let's Go Somewhere,* published by the Third World Press.

S. E. ANDERSON: Born August 16, 1943, in Bedford-Stuyvesant. Attended Lincoln University in Pennsylvania, and did grad work in mathematics. He is on the Advisory Board of the Drum and Spear Press and *Black Scholar* magazine and is currently teaching at the College of Old Westbury, SUNY.

IMAMU AMIRI BARAKA: was born October 7, 1934, in Newark, New Jersey. He received his B.A. degree from Howard University and did graduate work at the New School for Social Research and Columbia University. Among his many works are: *Home, Tales, Black Magic Poems, Four Revolutionary Plays,* and *Raise, Race, Rays, Raze*—a book of essays, among others. He is currently involved with the Committee for a Unified Newark and is the spiritual force behind Spirit House and publisher of Jihad Publications.

ED BULLINS: is the resident playwright of New Lafayette Theater in Harlem. His published work includes five plays: *The Duplex,* and *Four Dynamite Plays,* and a book of short stories, *The Hungered One.* He is editor of *Black Theatre Magazine* and his poetry has appeared in the *Journal of Black Poetry, Black World,* and *New Black Poetry.*

STANLEY CROUCH: Born in 1945 in L.A. He is teaching in the Black Studies Center of the Claremont Colleges in California. He has a recording of poetry entitled *No Ambulances for No Niggers Tonight.*

RONDA MARIE DAVIS: chicago poet, Africanese name-reader, high school teacher. Member of Oh-BAH-See Writers' Workshop and Gwen Brooks Writers' Workshop for four years. Works published: "rip-off" by Broadside Press; "wine-dipped woman" and "suhmtymz" in *Negro Digest;* several poems in both *Nommo* (magazine of OBAC), and *Jump Bad* (anthology of Brooks workshop).

JACQUELINE EARLEY: is a native of Ohio. Born December 17, 1939, in Buffalo, New York. Education: High School. Now residing in NYC; self-taught and independently pursuing the study of dance, art, drama, poetry, yoga philosophy, psychology, astrology, herbalism, and mysticism.

MARI EVANS: Producer/director of a weekly half-hour television series "The Black Experience" in Indiana; she is Writer-in-Residence and assistant professor in Black Literature at Indiana University. Her Book *I*

Am A Black Woman was published in November 1970 by Wm. Morrow & Company.

NIKKI GIOVANNI: was born a Sagittarius in 1943. Her books include, *Black Feeling/Black Talk, Black Judgement, Re:Creation,* and *Night Comes Softly,* an anthology of Black Female Voices.

DAVID HENDERSON: was born in Harlem in 1942. He has had various jobs ranging from a union organizer and presser in a cleaning store to teaching at City College and poet-in-residence. Among his published books are *Felix of the Silent Forest* and *De Mayor of Harlem.*

MAE JACKSON: born in Earl, Arkansas, January 3, 1946, is the author of one volume of poetry *Can I Poet With You.* Is also a winner of the Black World Third Conrad Kent Award, 1969. Is a member of the Student National Coordinating Committee. Is the mother of a beautiful daughter, Njeri Ayoka Cruse, who was born in the spirit of Ralph E. Featherstone who was assassinated by the U.S.A. government in Bel Air, Maryland, March 9, 1970. My works have been published in *Black World, Essence, Journal of Black Poetry.* I am now in the process of developing short stories for young black children.

NORMAN JORDAN: at 33, poet and playwright, norman jordan has been anthologized in *Black Fire,* and in *The New Black Poetry;* he has also appeared in: *Freelance, Vibrations, Cricket, Journal of Black*

Poetry, Black World, Confrontation and others. His plays have been staged in San Diego, Cleveland and New York. He is currently playwright-in-residence at Karamu.

GYLAN KAIN: presently working with The Original Last Poets and my new group called The Blue Guerilla which is a combination of poetry and black music. I'm also lecturing at colleges throughout the country. My play, *Epitaph to a Coagulated Trinity,* is being published in an anthology of black plays.

KALI: is a fifth grade student at P.S. 188 in Manhattan. She is the author of *Poems of Kali* published in 1970 by Doubleday and has written an article in *Redbook Magazine,* December 1970, about Christmas. Along with her sister, Chandra, she co-edits *Child's Play Magazine.* Her interests include: singing, dancing, fishing, playing with dolls and pretending. She would like to be a midwife in the future. She is currently working on a collection of short stories.

KEORAPETSE KGOSITSILE: was born in Johannesburg, South Africa, and has been in exile since 1961. His works include: *Spirits Unchained, My Name is Afrika,* and *For Melba.* In 1969, he received the Conrad Kent Rivers Memorial Award presented by *Black World* Magazine.

DON L. LEE: is the publisher of Third World Press and is currently writer-in-residence at Howard University. His books of poetry include: *Directionscore, Don't Cry, Scream,* and *We Walk the Way of the New*

World. His books of criticism, *Dynamite Voices,* are his most recent publications.

FELIPE LUCIANO: born a Sagittarian, the 24th of November '47 to 2 black Puerto Ricans. Moms says she put all her vitamins into me for 9 months. Raised in El Barrio—112th St. Poh people are mo-bile too so we lived in ever ghetto in N.Y. and L.A.; (Brownsville, L. Island City, Bushwick, Black Harlem, Spanish Harlem, East Los Angeles (Hollerbech), etc. Went to public schools mainly in New York. Loved school. Loved the streets. Busted for a gang-fight in '64. Got a pound. Served 2, upstate in Coxsachie (the name of the joint epitomizes the quality of the rehabilitation). Jail changed my life. Was a nice kid who cried watching army pictures. Came out a revolutionary but didn't know it. Went to Queens College; became politically active. Joined Last Poets, then co-founded The Young Lords Organization. Then the Young Lords Party in '69, along with every Puerto Rican in this city, particularly El Barrio. Was Chairman until August '70. Demoted over bullshit that looked political but didn't smell that way. Resigned my position in September. Now teaching, writing, lecturing and enjoying the lull before the next storm.

CLARENCE MAJOR: was born December 31, 1936, Atlanta, Georgia. Attended schools in Chicago; grew up in New York. His most recent titles are *Symptoms and Madness* published by Corinth Books, *Private Line,* a Paul Breman Ltd. of London publication, *The Cotton Club,* published by Broadside

Press and *Swallow the Lake,* which won the 1970 National Council of the Arts Award. The poems in this book are a part of a new collection.

AMUS MOR: has recorded his poetry, "The Bird Song," with The Association of Creative Musicians in Chicago. He is currently working on a novel and developing Black Psychoanalysis, The Psychology of Fascism. He was on the faculty at Prairie State Jr. College, in Chicago Heights, teaching Afro-American Art and directed the Black Cultural Center at the University of Massachusetts until "I decided that there was little possible relevant work that can be done inside the 'system' . . ."

LARRY NEAL: was born in 1937 in Atlanta, Georgia, and was reared in Philadelphia. He received a B.A. from Lincoln University and did graduate work at the University of Pennsylvania. He is an editor of *The Cricket* and a contributing editor of *Journal of Black Poetry.* Two forthcoming books are *Hoodoo Hollerin Bebop Ghosts,* a book of poetry, and *The Rise of Black Consciousness in the Sixties,* a book of essays.

DAVID NELSON: one of the Original Last Poets is widely known for his poem, "Die, Nigguh." Born in Detroit, he is currently working on his Ph.D. in Psychology at Teachers College, Columbia University. He has written a book of poetry, *Black Impulse,* which was published by Drum Publications.

"ARTHUR PFISTER": (brought to u by the makers of BLK/ARTSOUTH) "Born"—Sept. 20, 1949

REALLY Born–with my first taste of gumbo
in this debull infested jumbo
(m' poem-de-foist . . . du-duhhh)
ATTENDED–2 years of what was called "college" at
TUSKEGEE INSTITUTE
TUSKEGEE INSTITUTE, ALA. 36088
p.s.–like de udder dude,
i   came home from college
with my   gasoline   can . . .
(THE RADICALIZATIONALY BLACKENIZING OF BROTHER
BIGFOOT   BY   A   SOUTHERN/EEEEEEEEGROCOLLEGE
. . . . du-duhh agin)
RECEIVED–a VERY pale degree of M.A. in "Creative
Writing" from the John Hopkins University in Balto. Md.)
ACCOMPLISHMENTS–1) gave a kitten a home . . . . .
2) read jerry rubins first book
& didn't even or EVER
bother to comment on it
. . .
3) took a sister out 12 times &
didn't try to do "IT" . . .
4) made up a joke (a quip, or
what-have-u) about Mrs.
Santa being a relative clause
(nobody understood it!)
5) tried to write an autobio-
graphical sketch that at least
wdn't bore u . . .
(YAWN . . . capitol
DU-UHHHHH
. . . DE
N
D . . . .

CLARENCE REED: worked with the Black Arts Theater in Harlem. His book, *Forever Tears,* was published by Jihad Publications He was a member of the Harlem Black Panther Party.

CAROLYN RODGERS: Pioneer member of OBAC (Organization of Black American Culture), Gwen Brooks Writers' Workshop. Poems, essays, short stories, book reviews have appeared in a number of periodicals and anthologies. Anthologies: *We Speak as Liberators, Natural Process, Macmillan's Book of Short Black Stories.* Published two volumes of poetry: *Paper Soul, Songs of a Blackbird.* One Broadside: "Now Ain't That Love" and two foldovers, "Poem for Flip Wilson" and "2 Love Raps." Poetry published in *Black World, Journal of Black Poetry,* and *Nation Magazine.* Won first Conrad Kent Rivers Writing Award, in 1968. In 1970, I won the Poet Laureate Award of the Society of Midland Authors and also received a National Endowment of the Arts grant.

SONIA SANCHEZ: blk/woman/mother/poet/playwright/ teacher who tries to teach the truth. Author of 3 volumes of poetry: *Homecoming, We a BaddDDD People, It's a New Day (poems for young brothas and sistuhs).* At work on a fourth volume called *A Blues Book Fo Blue/Blk/Magical Women.* Author of 3 plays: *The Bronx is Next, Sister Son/Ji, Uh Huh; But How Do it Free Us?* Am also working on a novel. about me. us. Blk/woman/women. Some badDDDD mothas, who can only thru helping & loving each of other like sistuhs, git baddDDDER. Yeh!

WELTON SMITH: was born, with grave reservations, in Houston, Texas, in 1940. He promptly moved to San Francisco and was raised there. He has written a book of poems, *Penetration*, a play, *The Roach Riders*, a dance/voice piece, *The Adventures of Holy Ghost*, and a book of research, *The Art of Marahuana Ceremony as Performed on the Lower East Side of Manhattan, A.D. 1950–1980: A Primary Account of Ritual Among Indigenous and Emigre Pot-Heads by a Black Nationalist of Leisure and Genius.*

RICHARD W. THOMAS: Born 1939, Detroit, Michigan. Attended Miller High School, 1953–57. Served in Marine Corps, 1957–60. B.A. and M.A. in History at Michigan State University. Instructor, Center for Urban Affairs, M.S.U.

Published poems in magazines: *Volume 63* (University Waterloo), *Zeitgeist, New City, World Order, Red Cedar Review, Negro Digest, Colloquy.* Poems in anthologies: *Black Fire, Nine Black Poets, A Galaxy of Black Writing, Michigan Signatures* and *The Poetry of the Negro.*

JAMES W. THOMPSON: a Sagittarian from Detroit, Michigan: has been the Georgia Douglas Johnson of *First Avenue* for the past eight years maintaining *open house* for artists in various fields: poets, painters, dancers, choreographers, photographers, musicians, and writers. Dance reviewer for *The Feet.* My poems and short stories have appeared in various magazines and anthologies. Volume of early poems, *First Fire*, published by Paul Breman Ltd., London, England. Second volume, *Fire in the Flesh,* scheduled for publication by FIRE PUBlications sometime in 1972. Broadsides of two poems: "You Are Alms" and "For My Brother Charles" published by FIRE publications.

ASKIA MUHAMMAD TOURÉ: writer-activist, lecturer in Black Studies. Editor-at-Large of the *Journal of Black Poetry.* Widely published in major journals, *Black World, Freedomways, Liberator,* and *Soulbook.* And the anthologies, *The Poetry of the Negro—* L. Hughes & A. Bontemps, *Black Fire—*L. Jones & L. P. Neal, *Black Nationalism in America, Black Arts,* and *Natural Process.* Bro. Touré currently conducts a writer's worshop for undergraduate students at Columbia University.

QUINCY TROUPE: 28 years young, Leo. Born in NYC. Raised in St. Louis, Missouri. Attended Grambling College. Was a member of the Watts Writers. Edited *Watts Poets & Writers* (1968). Published in *Black World, Essence, Umbra, World Order, Sumac, Mundus Artium, Soul Illustrated,* anthologized in *The New Black Poetry,* edited by Clarence Major (1969). *We Speak as Liberators; Young Black Poets* edited by Orde Coombs (1970). *New Black Voices* edited by Abraham Chapman (1971). *New Directions* 22 edited by James Laughlin (1970) Newest collection of poetry, *Embryo, Poems From 1967–1971,* will be published by Barlenmir House in the spring of 1972. Is the editor of *Confrontation: A Journal of Third World Literature.* Teaches Third World Literature at Richmond College, Staten Island, N.Y., & at Ohio University, in Athens, Ohio. Lives in New York City.

About the Editor

WOODIE KING, JR., was born July 27, 1936, and raised in Detroit. He is currently the Artistic Director for the Henry Street Settlement, and the Founder and Co-director of the New Federal Theater. From 1965 to 1970 he was the Cultural Arts Director for the Mobilization for Youth in New York City where several films under its auspices received the Venice Festival Award and the International Film Critics Award among others.

Mr. King has also produced several plays such as *Black Quartet, Slaveship* by LeRoi Jones, *In New England Winters* by Ed Bullins and J. E. Franklin's *Black Girl.* He was also the producer of the three-day poetry festival from which this book evolved.

For his work in directing he received the John Hay Whitney Fellowship 1965–1966, and was a consultant to the Arts and Humanities board of the Rockefeller Foundation. Mr. King is also a free-lance writer and editor.